Mallory Meets His Match

Book 3 of the Kevin Mallory Series

Thomas Keech

Real
Nice Books
Baltimore, Maryland

Copyright © 2024 Thomas W. Keech
All rights reserved.

No part of this publication may be reproduced, stored in, or introduced into a retrieval system, or transmitted, in any form or by any means (electronic, mechanical, photocopying, recording, or otherwise), without the proper written permission of the copyright owner, except that a reviewer may quote brief passages in a review.

ISBN: 979-8-9885034-2-2 Hardback
ISBN: 979-8-9885034-3-9 Paperback
ISBN: 979-8-9885034-4-6 Ebook
ISBN: 979-8-9885034-5-3 Audiobook

Library of Congress Control Number 2024901586

Published by

Real
Nice Books
11 Dutton Court, Suite 606
Baltimore, Maryland 21228
www.realnicebooks.com

Publisher's note: This is a work of fiction. Names, characters, places, institutions, and incidents are entirely the product of the author's imagination or are used fictitiously, and any resemblance to actual persons, living or dead, or to events, incidents, institutions, or places is entirely coincidental.

Cover photo credit: Shutterstock.
Set in Minion Pro.

For Chuck

Also by Thomas Keech:

The Crawlspace Conspiracy
Prey for Love
Hot Box in the Pizza District
Doc Doc Zeus: A Novel of White Coat Crime
Stacey in the Hands of an Angry God
A New God in Town
Mallory's Manly Methods
Mallory Goes to Therapy

Chapter 1: Our Hero's Dilemma

Mallory was beginning to understand the sinister forces that were relegating him to such a below-average life. He was thirty-two years old and didn't have a family, a decent job, a presentable apartment, a car, a wife, a girlfriend, or even a pet. He had always suspected that his multiple failures at multiple entry level jobs in the last fifteen years could not be just coincidence. And now he had a new friend who was teaching him exactly who was keeping him economically at the bottom of the barrel, socially a pariah, and romantically limited to the cheapest porn site he could find.

The solutions he had sought out, followed, and sometimes paid for in the past year had never really gotten to the heart of the problem. His rage against the hedge fund tycoons who were running UniCast Cable had gotten him nowhere. In fact, those same tycoons were now planning on firing thousands of employees nationwide to make the company more attractive as a takeover prospect. The dating advice he had gotten from Manly Man, his internet guru, had led him into failure after failure with women. Even the glimmer of happiness he had chased after in his group therapy meetings had faded.

Kathie was another of his failures. He had rescued her from a pathetic lesbian relationship with Nell, their co-worker, but that hadn't led to anything but a free ride to work every day and an occasional quick lunch out of the office. She was tall, blonde, hot, and hetero, and with a seemingly different take on life. It was taking him longer to figure her out than any woman he had ever known. She shared his disdain for UniCast but, unlike him, she excelled at her job. She had told him once that she admired his talent for saving other employees' jobs, but she hadn't said anything that nice to him in weeks.

His co-worker, Nell, who occupied the cubicle right next to him, was holding a grudge against him, falsely blaming him for stealing Kathie from her. His supervisor, Harrison, was fully aware that Mallory did almost no work at all in his position as Customer Service Assistant – even though he was stalemated from doing anything about it by Mallory's customer satisfaction ratings. At least Kathie, who was responsible for those ratings, made sure that Mallory's were always among the highest of any employee in Harrison's division.

He hated the job, but he was too demoralized to look for another one. He was humiliated that Kathie was treating him like a charity case. Often, late at night, lying on his sofa bed in the darkness of his one-room efficiency apartment, eyeing the little red and green lights that blinked at random from somewhere under the tangle of computer wires on the other side of the room, he wondered why nobody had ever loved him. But now he was getting some answers, thanks to Spike.

Spike, the twenty-year-old waiter at the Dough and Go, Mallory's favorite restaurant, was his sole source of knowledge about what was happening in the neighborhood, the country, and the world. But Spike's jaunty, superior attitude toward the workaday world, and especially toward his father, the Greek immigrant owner and manager of the restaurant, had changed since he had been rejected for admission to business school at State. He no longer openly bragged about his soccer skills, his Facebook followers, his bright future in the world of finance. He spoke in a lower voice now, often looking over his shoulder to make sure his father wasn't listening.

Mallory walked a mile and a half down the side of the highway to the Dough and Go, as he did almost every evening. His face was flushed from the long hike in the cool but humid September air. Now that his Escalade had been repossessed, he had to walk everywhere that Kathie didn't drive him. He could no longer afford to wear the suits that had given him a modicum of respect from the women at work. But at least he was no longer fearful of people in hoodies, since he was now one of them. He arrived hot, sweaty and hungry, and not in the mood to hear more of Spike's theories. Spike took his order and soon laid a thick ceramic plate piled with two burgers and fries down on the table in front of him. Mallory stared at the plate and emitted a soft moan of anticipation. But Spike had lately begun the startling new habit of sitting down across from Mallory in the booth after he served him.

"Have you been following that website, *The Real Honest to God's Truth*, like we talked about? I've started commenting on that website."

"I don't think I want to think about that stuff today," Mallory began. As he fingered the burger in front of him, his mouth contorted itself in almost orgasmic anticipation.

Spike told him he had begun an internet campaign of revenge against State's School of Business – and also, he now told Mallory, against the whole educational establishment in the country. He bragged that he'd posted hundreds of comments about it on *God's Truth* and he was becoming popular there. "And my ideas are going viral. Four hundred and fifty followers on my own Facebook page, 150 on my X. And I'm starting to trend on Instagram, too."

"Are you doing all this yourself?"

"I have some friends I met on Facebook who think the same way. People need to know how the system locks out people like us. I'll spend as much time on this as I have to."

"Right." Mallory nodded as he tried to avoid eye contact. He wanted to get to his food. He was afraid Spike would start showing him his comments. Mallory didn't like to read, even if there were pictures involved. And Spike's comments always seemed to simply repeat what he was reading on *The Real Honest to God's Truth* on his own computer every night. But Spike would not keep quiet.

"I'm the most popular commentator on *God's Truth*. And guess what? A lot of my comments are about you! You're a hero now!"

The Real Honest to God's Truth was the first non-porn, non-Manly Man website Mallory had ever frequented. He had been alarmed to read there about the frightening groups of deviants who had decided that they were the normal people and that, from now on, people like him would have to be shoved aside. But Spike had taught him that he shouldn't be afraid. Knowing the enemy, he said, was the first step toward putting the perverts back in their place, and *God's Truth* was the best place to find out about the enemy. Mallory seethed with outrage every night as the website revealed how far his economic status, his rights, and even his pronouns, were being taken away. But Mallory hadn't realized that Spike posted his own comments on *God's Truth*. And he was terrified now that Spike was posting about him.

"What do you mean, *hero?*"

"Take a look!" Spike pushed his phone in front of his face.

MAN DEFIES SWAT TEAM, RESCUES CAT FROM LESBIAN TRIANGLE. *Congratulations to Kevin Mallory, a true American hero who rescued his dear pet at the risk of his life.*

"That's not what happened." Mallory's memory of events, especially those that were traumatic to him, had never been very good, but he was sure he hadn't rescued the cat that day, and there was no lesbian triangle, and he remembered he had ended up face down on the courthouse parking lot with a SWAT team member's foot on his neck. "You've got that all mixed up."

"No, man, you are a hero. And I want everyone on *God's Truth* to know it."

"I'm not really sure this whole thing is a good idea."

Mallory wasn't sure of anything. He had briefly been intrigued by the revelations on *The Real Honest to God's Truth* about the web of conspiracies to rewrite all history so regular people like him would be blamed for oppressing every non-white, non-hetero person who ever had a bad day. But he had not yet gotten up the nerve to mention these conspiracies out loud to anyone. "I'm not sure I want people to know about the cat incident," he said now. "I apologized for that, you know."

"Apologizing – that was a mistake. But I can understand why you did that. They came after you. They come after anyone who stands up and speaks the truth."

Mallory didn't remember anyone coming after him. And he was certain he hadn't rescued Koko. A week after the incident at the courthouse, he'd given that cat, which he had stolen, back to Nell. But it was true that he was barely holding onto his low-level job, slowly going bankrupt, paying money he couldn't afford just to get a moment's joy out of watching third-rate porn star Simone de Boudoir on his computer at night. He recognized that *The Real Honest to God's Truth* might be pointing him in the right direction, but he wasn't sure he wanted to go there if he had to put out of his mind everything that had really happened at the courthouse.

"But I don't remember doing anything like what you said," he insisted now.

After quickly looking over his shoulder to make sure his father wasn't listening, Spike leaned across the table toward him. His stare was intense, and he seemed to be looking beyond Mallory somehow. The reflection from the red neon sign in the window made his eyes glow as if he were staring into a burning bush.

"It doesn't matter what *details* you might *think* you remember, I'm sure I got to the *basic truth* of the matter. People can't understand these basic truths if they get lost in the details. And look!" He showed Mallory his phone again. Mallory didn't understand what the numbers on the screen meant, so Spike explained. "Eight hundred and sixty-four people liked my comments. People are starting to know what you've done, and to appreciate your bravery."

"Uh, okay. Are your cinnamon buns fresh today?"

*** ***

Mallory was so frightened about what Spike was saying about him on *God's Truth* that he put off telling Kathie anything about this. It was alarming that Spike himself had only about 450 followers on Facebook and 270 on Instagram and 150 on X, but now he had commented so often on *The Real Honest to God's Truth* that his theories were being liked by over 800 people. And Spike wasn't using any discretion at all in telling Mallory's story.

But Mallory then began to see the upside to this.

"You know, I'm kind of famous now." He was riding to work with Kathie in her little pickup truck. He was constantly bewildered by his long-legged, green-eyed co-worker with her massive crown of blonde curls – and her casual but persistent concern for his welfare. She acted so down to earth and practical he'd half given up on seducing her, though he held steadfast to his dream that she'd be wild in bed.

"Oh, yeah?" Her voice was dismissive. She wasn't the kind of woman who felt her job was to cheer up everybody around her.

"No. Really. I've got thousands of hits on social media." Mallory wasn't really sure what this meant, but he'd heard this phrase before. "People are saying I'm a hero."

"Oh yeah? Why's that?"

"It's about that thing at the courthouse. The SWAT team and all."

"You were a *hero* there?" she said, her voice now dripping with doubt.

"That's what everybody says."

"Hm."

"Anyway, if you'll look at this website, and look at the comments, you'll see all my followers."

Mallory had never used Facebook or Instagram except to look at sexy pictures of teenage girls. Lately he'd found that TikTok was even better for that. But as he gradually dug deeper into the internet, past those social media sites, and past his porn site, and past Manly Man, and finally into *God's Truth*, Mallory felt himself being pulled in two different directions. He was thrilled to discover on *God's Truth* the hidden forces that were condemning him to the half-life he was living now. And he was glad to find out there was a whole community of people online who were as angry as he was about what was happening. They called themselves "God's Martyrs." Mallory was thrilled to find out it didn't cost anything to join, and that there were absolutely no qualifications he had to meet in order to become a Martyr. He didn't feel quite so alone once he typed in his name and made himself a member. But, at the same time, God's Martyrs could do nothing to stop what was happening to him personally. None of his friends, he was sure, would really understand the reasons he was being constantly forced further and further down the economic and social ladders. He was afraid he would continue his downhill slide forever, right in front of their eyes, without them ever realizing that he wasn't to blame for it at all.

"Maybe you should follow me, too" he tried now.

"Follow you on what?" Kathie asked.

"I don't know. The internet or something. Just follow me."

Her glance over at him seemed sincere. "Kevin, we drive together to work every day. We talk while we're at work most days. I drive you home every day. I know everything about you that makes any difference to me. What could I possibly gain by seeing some post of yours online?"

"You're not going to follow me online?"

"You need to get offline and get your act together. You seem to have plenty of spare time at night. You should get a second job."

Mallory was confused. Spike was always telling him how important his online presence was, but Kathie didn't think so. And he needed more than anything the chance to get closer to her. He didn't know who to believe. He had never thought it worthwhile to compare the merits of two different people's suggestions. Every choice he had made in his entire life had been guided only by his own instincts, which were pretty much limited to either primal fear or the hope for some immediate pleasure.

He yearned for a closer connection with Kathie. He had recurring dreams that she was coming around. But Spike was offering him a once in a lifetime chance of escaping his life sentence as an underpaid UniCast drone. He had never before had to choose between two things he needed so much.

"You're right," he told Kathie now. "I probably just need to get a second job."

*** ***

"You're right," he told Spike that night. "Let's keep it up. Let's stop those WOKES and LGBTQs, and the plusses, from destroying our hard-won lifestyle."

Chapter 2: Details, Details

Spike was thrilled. "We have to keep posting. We'll have thousands of followers soon! We'll go viral!"

"But, what will I put out there for people to follow?"

"Your story, of course. Here, hand me your phone."

CAT HERO KEVIN MALLORY SHAFTED BY MANAGEMENT. *UniCast Cable Company won't respond to controversy about failure to promote long-term, highly rated, white employee.*

"What?" Mallory was puzzled by Spike's post – *his* post now. "I never applied for any promotion."

"*Details*. Listen to me, Kevin. Forget the details. We have to get to the point, get to the real truth. The real truth is, you didn't apply for the promotion because you knew there was not the slightest chance you would get it. The whole system is set up to replace truly talented, regular people like you and me – all so that so-called 'underserved' people can be given for free the things that regular people work all our lives for. If you study it closely, like I have, you'll see that while the 'underserved' are being *overserved*, you and I will soon be reduced to crawling on our knees to them just to feed our families."

"Our *families*?" Mallory had never really had a family except for his mother, and he hadn't spoken to her in months. And he knew Spike was single, living with his parents, and was not feeding anybody's family.

"It doesn't matter if we have actual families. Soon there won't even be any such thing as a *family* anyway, Spike went on. "It's already happening. School children are already being taught to celebrate boys who change into girls and girls who change into boys. Regular kids are being corrected for calling themselves "normal" because teachers believe there is no such thing as normal anymore. Kids are taught that normal families are a thing of the past."

Details, Details

"Oh my God!"

Mallory was as confused as he was frightened by Spike's observations. Over the next few weeks, he got a lot of responses on social media, but it was all so overwhelming he let Spike handle all the back and forth. He was shocked to learn he had somehow created his own audience on *The Real Honest to God's Truth* and had posted fifteen opinions already. He was afraid to read them.

But Nell had read them. "What is this crap you're posting about me? I ought to sue you!"

He had to guess. "Is this about Koko the cat? You have to admit you killed him."

She gave him a cold, pasty-faced stare as she lectured him through gritted teeth. "You know that's not the truth. He died during an operation. At the vet's. I was concerned about his health. I was paying for it. And what does my being a lesbian have to do with abusing cats, anyway? You know I loved Koko, and all my other cats, and all my dogs."

"Uh, maybe I went too far in what I said." But Mallory instantly regretted admitting he could be in the wrong. What had gotten into him? Admitting he was wrong? What kind of slippery slope was he sliding down now?

"You're damn right you did! Take all that stuff down immediately, or I really will sue you."

Later that day, Spike assured Mallory that he had taken all references to cat brutality down from all the sites. "Okay, let's lay off the cats for a while. We have over fifteen hundred followers now on Facebook and X combined! And I have an artist friend who's creating a cartoon image of you for Instagram and TikTok. We're beginning to be heard. Let's focus on the important stuff and keep going!"

"I agree." Mallory wasn't sure what the important stuff was. He now knew he had been oppressed, treated unfairly, his whole life. And here was Spike, a star athlete and internet prodigy, kept out of business school because all the spaces had been taken by LGBTQ-plusses and WOKEs; and Spike was now stifled, condemned to working twenty hours a week for his ignorant Greek immigrant father who kept a more watchful eye on him than ever before.

"At this rate, we'll have five thousand followers by the end of the month!"

"Great." Mallory was terrified.

*** ***

Harrison sat so stiffly behind his desk that Mallory thought his supervisor looked scared. Ever since the Ms. Marcie incident, Harrison had eyed his every move with suspicion. Now he made a point of taking down in writing everything Mallory said. This tactic was truly disturbing to Mallory, who had always counted on the free flow of his imagination to re-create to his own advantage any conversation he had with his boss.

Ms. Marcie, Harrison's office assistant, had been called into the room as well. Because of the recent imbroglio between Mallory and Ms. Marcie on one side and Harrison on the other, Harrison now made a point of never speaking to either of them alone. Six weeks before, under pressure from upper management to cut costs, Harrison, in a panic, had cruelly threatened to fire Ms. Marcie when she arrived late for work one day. She had come to Mallory for help. Mallory had sat quietly next to her and encouraged her as she filled out the complaint form, explaining that she had a flat tire on the way to work and the towing service she called had been slow to respond. Then, as soon as she left the room, he threw her complaint in the trash. Mallory was sure nobody would be interested in such a boring story, so he typed up a new one that he was sure would get Corporate's attention.

Ms. Marcie had been as shocked as anybody when the corporate human resources investigator from Houston read the complaint out loud in the subsequent emergency meeting. Mallory had replaced Ms. Marcie's boring story with a tale of Harrison taking Ms. Marcie's shoes and requiring her to crawl around the office in search of them. Then, Mallory added, Harrison had over a period of weeks gradually required her to take off more and more items of clothing. Mallory had ended the complaint with what he thought of as a masterpiece of fiction, a lurid description of Harrison prancing around the office wearing Ms. Marcie's panties over his own pants.

No one in that meeting had believed that Harrison would do these things to Ms. Marcie, or that Ms. Marcie would go along with these shenanigans for even a minute. Everyone knew that this version was false, and that Mallory had authored it. He had found himself unable to return their stares. He had resigned himself to being fired on the spot. But just at that point, Ms. Marcie had saved him by coming up with an even more ridiculous story, blaming the whole thing on her poor handwriting – a story which no one really believed either, but which was good enough for the corporate investigator to go back to Texas and happily close the books on the whole thing as an unfortunate misunderstanding.

But, without question, everyone in the corporate office in Houston was still gossiping about this. Harrison looked like an idiot for presiding over an office where the employees were so bold as to make up a ridiculous story like that – and get away with it. And he couldn't afford to look like a weak link just as UniCast was trying to cut employees so it could be taken over by the Everdine hedge fund.

Speaking to Mallory and Ms. Marcie together would be even more dangerous than speaking to either of them alone, so Harrison called Peggy, Ms. Marcie's office mate, into his office also. Peggy, who didn't seem as meek as Ms. Marcie, sighed and rolled her large, protruding eyes at her boss. Evidently, she didn't think being a witness to every meeting between her boss and Ms. Marcie was a good use of her time. She did perk up when she saw that Mallory was there also, but then her expression turned sour once again when Mallory took the only empty chair left.

"I was just in the middle of ...."

"I know, Peggy," Harrison cut her off. "But I need you at this meeting. Sit down, everybody."

Peggy swiveled her head slowly from side to side as if she expected a chair for her to magically appear.

"Oh. Oh." Harrison's voice was apologetic. He stood up and rolled his big leather chair in her direction. "Here, take mine. Let's get started. This won't take long, I hope." Peggy looked like she also hoped this wouldn't be a long meeting.

"This may take quite a while, I'm afraid," Mallory intoned into the fractious silence. "A lot of people have been complaining to me about you. They say you're cold, unfriendly. *Curt*, even. Everybody thinks you're looking for a reason to fire them. You're making everybody miserable. That's harassment on a grand scale."

Harrison sniffed. "I've always tried to be courteous to every employee. If anyone has a problem with my demeanor, they should come to me directly." But his voice was weak.

"Let's face it, Harrison, nobody's going to come to you directly. Not after you created this hostile work environment. After the Ms. Marcie complaint, half the people in this office think you're cruel, and the other half think you're a pervert."

Harrison's face dropped. Ms. Marcie's face turned red at that last word. Mallory smiled and turned to see what Peggy's reaction was, but she just screwed up her lips like she was just waiting for the whole thing to be over with. Harrison then leaned over his desk, grabbed a pen, and apparently started writing down every word that Mallory had just said. This process was so awkward, and was taking so long, that Peggy volunteered to take the notes.

"Good. Thank you, Peggy. Mr. Mallory, we'll deal with your issue later. I called this meeting to give you a warning, Mr. Mallory. This warning comes all the way from corporate. You are posting false statements about the company on social media, postings that are being followed by hundreds, maybe thousands of people. This is a violation of your basic duty of loyalty to the company ...."

"*Loyalty*? You've got to be kidding."

"Yes, loyalty. Look in your company handbook, Mr. Mallory. And you've also been spreading lies about a co-employee …."

"Nell."

"See? You're admitting it right now. Make sure you write that down, Peggy."

"I thought I took those postings about Nell down."

"Got that, too, Peggy? Mr. Mallory, maybe you don't know how the internet works …."

"*Of course* I know how the internet works." Mallory knew almost nothing about the internet, but he didn't like it when his expertise in any area was challenged.

"People can pick up anything you post and re-post it over and over." Harrison's voice was shaking in anger. "It can live on forever. You'll never be able to erase those comments about Nell, or the company." Ms. Marcie leaned forward, her hand to her mouth, obviously searching for words to calm her usually mild-mannered boss. But the words didn't come.

Mallory had never personally posted anything on the internet except his credit card number and a few questions to Manly Man. He was shocked to think that the internet was keeping a permanent record of everything that Spike was now posting in his name. He usually counted on people forgetting what he said ten seconds after he had gotten what he wanted out of the conversation. Even here, with nothing but Peggy's old-fashioned pen poised over her old-fashioned notepad to take down his statement, he was afraid to go on. There was a full minute of silence before he responded. His voice was shaky at first but grew stronger as he ventured into the familiar territory of his imagination.

"I already settled with Nell. Tell the company to sue me! I've never posted anything that wasn't true, and I'll defend my opinions to the death!"

Mallory Meets His Match

*** ***

It occurred to Mallory that he might want to check up on what Spike was now posting on social media sites in his name. The matter took on more urgency the next morning, when Nell slammed a heavy folder down onto his desk, knocking his coffee over into his cinnamon buns and ruining his breakfast.

"They're still up! Your posts accusing me of killing Koko are still up!"

Mallory jumped back, whacking his chair into the back of Nell's cubicle, but not quickly enough to keep the coffee-and-cinnamon mush from dripping onto his pants. He felt the hot water seeping onto his legs. Nell had assaulted him! No matter what Spike had posted on the internet, he felt they were even now. He didn't owe Nell any explanation at all. But he did want to demonstrate his new knowledge to her. "Don't you understand about the internet, Nell? Those things get sent around. It takes time to clear them all up." He was amazed at how stupid she was.

"You told me last week you had taken everything down." He noticed she was letting her attractive, straight-cut bob grow out now. He had once believed she had cut her hair in that sleek style just to attract him. What a fool he had been! But now, he enjoyed seeing her go to seed. It made it easier for him to deal with her.

"Yes, *I* took everything down on *my* end, but it takes a few days for all the *correspondents* to follow up on that. They have to follow all the *internet protocols* first." Mallory hoped she wouldn't ask what these words meant. She did seem appropriately confused for a second – but she knew him too well to stay confused for long.

"Don't lie to me. You put up a new post just yesterday, the one where you said Koko was fatally injured when I tried to mate him with a German Shepherd."

Mallory laughed. He had not seen that post yet, but he couldn't

19

help admiring Spike's creativity.

Nell mouth dropped open. "You don't even know what's being posted? You hired a bot to keep trashing me? I'm going to sue you for every penny you have."

"I don't *have* a penny, Nell." Mallory put a hand in his pocket and emptied its entire contents onto a dry part of his desk. "Here, look. Here's half of a broken comb. Here's a Dough and Go Frequent Eater Rewards coupon. Here's a licorice gumdrop in the shape of Mario. That's everything I have. Take it all. It's yours."

Nell now spoke through clenched teeth. "I will find a way to make you sorry, if it's the last thing I ever do."

Chapter 3: Repercussions of Things Past

I want to meet with you, but somewhere else.

Mallory ignored Kathie's instructions and cruised through the aisles to her worksite on the opposite side of the building. When he got there, he was shocked to see another woman crammed into her cubicle with her. They seemed to be sharing the same computer. There was no place for him to sit. Mallory didn't know what to do. He didn't recognize the other woman. When Kathie finally caught sight of him, she motioned him away and followed him out into the corridor. Then she walked right past him and kept walking fast down the corridor, past the break room, past another bank of cubicles, around more turns, through the lobby, and outside to the parking lot. Mallory was out of breath by the time she stopped next to her truck.

"I didn't want you to see that," she started.

"See what? By the way, what's that woman doing in your office?"

"Let's go get a drink."

Although Nell's Cheer Committee was banned from the Pirate Bar, Mallory, who had paid for all the damages from last year's holiday party with his credit card, was still welcome. The day manager, Leila, was not there when he arrived with Kathie. Mallory was glad about that, as he could usually focus his manly attention on only one attractive woman at a time. But the large pirate bartender was there, black eyepatch still in place, staring warily at the couple with his other eye. But he seemed to mellow when Kathie walked up to the bar and ordered the drinks for their table.

"Are you going to tell me what that other woman was doing in your cubicle?" Mallory surprised himself by remembering that other woman at all. Normally, his recall of meeting any woman over the age of forty was as evanescent as gas passed in a strong wind.

Kathie took a long drink of her bourbon.

"It's just computer shit. I don't want to talk about it." She seemed more interested in drinking than talking. She signaled the pirate bartender for another. Mallory started to worry about who would pay. But when her second drink came, she just put it down and leaned forward with her elbows on the table. She was breathing heavily, but not in the aroused way that Mallory would have preferred. She seemed angry.

"I can't work like this. I can't share an office with Meredith," she began again.

"Yeah. She doesn't seem too attractive. Does she smell, too?"

"Don't be gross." Kathie huffed. "It's not like that. She's actually pretty nice. But I can't get my work done if I'm constantly sharing my computer with her. How am I supposed to run the statistical operation when she's on my computer half the time? Not to mention there's no place to put our bags and shit."

Mallory thought it was his manly duty to come up with a solution for her problem. He slowly swirled his Margarita around in his glass while he focused on what she had said. Finally, it hit him. "Tell Harrison you need a computer of your own! Chub told me that UniCast made over $1.5 billion in profit last year. I think they can spare the money for a new computer for their chief regional statistician."

She took a sip of her new drink, sighed. "It's not a money problem. It's complicated. And embarrassing. I don't think you want to hear all the details."

She was right in thinking that he didn't want to hear all the details. He had always known he was constitutionally unfit for listening to other people's problems. But he was intrigued by Kathie. When they had both been on the Cheer Committee, she was the only woman who seemed to appreciate his ideas. She seemed to run her three-person statistical unit with the kind of calm managerial competence that Harrison seemed to lack. She had once helped save their co-employee Chub's job by posing as a programmer for two weeks, risking her own job so he could take time off to rescue his daughter. And he was sure she really liked men, even though, curiously, she didn't seem to be into him in that way.

"I would love to hear the details," he said, suddenly surprising himself.

"Oh. Okay." She looked at him with something he thought might be appreciation in her eyes. "It started with the cables. They say the new computers need a bundle of specialized cables, and UniCast has run out of those cables."

"Why don't they just order more?"

"They say they can't. They say they're on backorder. Supply chain problems, they say. They won't be in for six months or more. They say."

To the extent that Mallory was paying attention, it seemed like some kind of routine business problem, something so dull he couldn't imagine listening to any more of. But Kathie's expression tightened as she repeated those last words – *they say*. He then realized that Kathie was trying to tell him something more than what was in her actual words. He didn't know people could do that. She was the first person he had ever met who could communicate with him like that. He felt he had gained a new power of understanding, a power that Manly Man had never even spoken of. He suspected this new power would work only with her.

"What's the real story?" he challenged her. He sensed she would tell him the truth if she really liked him. He spoke with confidence in his own instincts, a confidence he had never before felt when speaking with a woman.

"Rhys Davies. In Building Management. He hates me. He screwed things up for me last month when he put one of my staff way down at the end of the corridor. I had to have a knock-down-drag-out talk with the Building Manager to get him moved back."

"You gonna do the same thing this time?"

"I can't. Not anymore. Rhys got promoted. Now he *is* the Building Manager."

Mallory had no experience in trying to solve workplace problems. Although he knew he was an expert in making up excuses for himself, distracting management from his misbehavior, and using a plethora of other personnel defensive maneuvers, he hadn't lately – or, perhaps, ever – been good at finding actual solutions for real problems. But he pondered over Kathie's problem for the rest of the afternoon anyway. That evening, he trekked down the edge of the highway to visit Spike and explain how Kathie was being screwed.

"Oh, man, that sucks."

Mallory was glad he got Spike's attention focused on Kathie before the young man started his glory stories about how he and Mallory were becoming internet darlings.

"The head of Building Management, Rhys, is dumping on my friend, Kathie. And our own boss, Harrison, is afraid to mess with Building Management."

"Isn't that the way it goes these days? Unless you're in some kind of elite or special group …."

Mallory cut him off. "Can't we do something about Kathie's problem?"

Spike met his eyes, for once. "Can't you see the conspiracy here? Haven't you learned anything from *The Real Honest to God's Truth*?"

"What? Just tell me."

"You told me that Nell's gay, right? And she had a gay thing going with Kathie, right? And then Kathie cut her off, right? That's how the LGBT-plusses are these days. They never let anything go. Anybody who crosses them will be punished."

"Omigod! Of course. It must be Nell behind this. She does hate Kathie now." He tapped a forefinger on the top of his burger roll. "She's gotten Rhys to hold up Kathie's new computer. It's LGBT revenge. Why didn't I see this myself?"

"Maybe you were too close to it to see the big picture. That's why you've got to keep up with *God's Truth*. And all the posts. Here, let me see your phone."

Vagina Vendetta: Lovelorn Lesbian Cuts Computer Cables to

Mallory Meets His Match

Licentious Lady ....

"No!" Mallory grabbed the phone before Spike could finish his post. He poked at the screen until he managed to erase the whole text. "Now you're getting Kathie into it, too. You gotta stop."

Spike spread his hands out like he was explaining something obvious. "We have over twelve hundred followers, over three thousand likes on every post lately. Give the people what they want. That's how you get noticed. That's how you get power. I can keep this up. We'll have ten thousand followers in a week, a hundred thousand in two weeks. Just let me do my thing."

Mallory took a nervous bite of his cinnamon bun and gulped it down with the dregs of his coffee. "Okay, I guess. But leave Kathie out of this."

Spike agreed to leave Kathie out of it, but he insisted that people were eating up his stories about Nell using her cats in bestial ways. They needed that kind of story to keep their audience growing at such an exponential rate, he said. Mallory was too exhausted by that time to disagree. He was also still furious with Nell for spilling coffee on his pants. He began the walk back home on the side of the highway that night, proud that he had discovered that it was Nell who was making Kathie's work life miserable. He would find a way to fix that. Then Kathie would realize that he was a player. Then maybe she would play with him. He was depressed that he would have only Simone de Boudoir's ecstatic screams for company that night. He suspected that Kathie was every bit the passionate female that Simone was. He was trying to hold onto that fantasy of having Kathie in his bed, but he decided he'd settle for her to come over just for a cup of coffee now – if he had any coffee.

*** ***

Kathie had told him not to call her at night, but she had never said not to come to her apartment in person. He walked the three miles to her building in the dark, took the elevator to the fifth floor and pushed the ornate button outside her door.

"Omigod! I told you not to contact me at night." She seemed as breathless as he was.

"Oh. You're doing some guy right now. I should have guessed."

"Shut up. People can hear you. There's no guy here." She looked up and down the hallway. "You can come in."

She told him he could sit down. He was relieved. He was tired, and his feet hurt. She sat down at the other end of the sofa, her long legs crossed in their pale blue jeans. She was wearing a tight, white blouse that was buttoned one button too short to allow him to focus on her face. How he wished he could touch her! She stretched her arms above her head, took in a deep breath, and yawned. He watched in wonder. But her eyes looked tired, and he didn't think she was thinking what he was thinking. He wondered what she had been doing. Her television wasn't on, and there was no video screen of any kind in sight. There weren't even any snacks on the coffee table. There was no clue about what she normally did at night. He was dying to ask her.

She suddenly jumped up and ran to the kitchen and brought him back a glass of water, explaining that she didn't have any beer in the apartment. Neither of them mentioned cognac, the liquor that Mallory had famously used in his many failed attempts to seduce women. He noticed that her movements were a little too quick, as if she were nervous. It certainly wasn't because she was afraid of him, but he allowed himself to dream that his manly powers were working a little, even with her. As much as he was dying for a kiss, a touch, any sign of affection from her, he had to admit to himself that Kathie didn't seem to be dying for anything, except maybe her computer cables.

"So, what's up?" She raised her eyebrows and gave him a quick conspiratorial smile. But then her cheerful demeanor quickly melted away. Mallory couldn't tell if she was afraid of him or bored with him, but he was sure her mood had something to do with him.

"I've been talking to Spike about your cable problem. He thinks it might be part of the conspiracy by Nell and the LGBTQ-plusses."

Kathie jerked herself upright. "I don't want to hear about it, Kevin. I'm sick of all this Spike talk and of all your conspiracy theories from *God's Roof* or whatever the hell it's called. What you need is a second job so you can start to pay your bills. You're wasting your time on all this crap."

Mallory shrunk back in his seat. He had never seen Kathie so worked up. But he told himself it was his time to be brave. "But these people have the answers to so many questions. Even your computer cable problem – they've figured it out."

Kathie huffed dismissively, but then she turned toward him. She then gently touched her fingertips to his wrist. He thought he saw a trace of something in her eyes. Was it frustration? Yearning for connection with him? He was stimulated beyond all reason. But he had learned that he had a lot to learn about her. "Kevin. I'm a simple person. I don't believe in all these conspiracies like you do. I can't live that way. Like I said, I think you should focus on getting a second job." She sat back. He couldn't help staring at her hand, which was now just resting on the sofa cushion. When he raised his gaze from her hand, he was surprised to see an embarrassed look in her eyes. She looked down, bit her lip in a prelude to a confession.

"You're a good friend. I should have told you this before. I've always known the reason I can't get any computer cables from Rhys. We used to live together, secretly. I kicked him out of the apartment a few months ago."

Mallory was stunned, and too upset to try to think any of this through. He'd always suspected that she'd had previous boyfriends, but the idea of her living with that creep Rhys cut him to the quick. He'd always dreamed he'd be the first real man she let into her life. He realized now that didn't make any sense. She was beautiful, smart, hot, friendly, and almost thirty. In all that time, there probably had been legions of men who went after her. He had been stupid for pretending to himself he was the only one who would be able to properly get her off. But now, he knew he'd be lucky if he could be the next in line.

"But what happened? I mean with Rhys."

"You know, when you live with somebody, you learn a lot about yourself. At least I did. Looking back on it, I'm not proud of the way I was with him."

"You cheated on him?"

"Do you think everything is about sex? No, I didn't cheat on him. But, you know that lie he is telling everybody about my computer cables? Well, that wasn't the first time he lied to me."

She offered to drive him back to his apartment. He was glad she had opened up to him about Rhys. He couldn't really see how a lie that was not about sex could ruin a relationship, but he decided to take her word for it. He wanted to invite her in, but he realized the enticement had to be something more than the chance to get a taste of his leftover cognac and go to bed with him on his fold-out sofa.

"I've been fixing the place up." He had just decided to do that in that very instant.

"Oh yeah?"

"Yeah. I figured the computer and screen and the router and all those wires and stuff, and that rickety wicker bench, were taking up half the room in the place. I'm going to get an actual chair if I can find one at Goodwill."

"Hmm." She didn't sound like she was impressed with his decorating plans. He looked over to see what she meant, but in the dim, wavering blue and pink light from her truck's touchscreen, he could see only her waterfall of corkscrewed hair. "That sounds like a worthwhile project," she finally begrudged him.

"It's just a tiny place," he admitted.

"Yeah. I hear you've got nothing but a sofa bed. Do you ever think about moving?"

"No. Why do you ask that?"

"I'm thinking about moving. I mean, I am moving. I can't afford to keep up that two-bedroom apartment on just my salary." She turned to him in the dim purplish light. "I wanted to ask you something about that." Mallory fought to suppress his excitement. Was this down-to-earth woman going to ask him to move in with her?

"Yes! The answer is yes."

"You don't know what the question is yet. I was wondering if you would help me move next Saturday."

He nodded, but then quickly got out of the car. The darkness in his own apartment matched his mood, and he could hardly bring himself to turn on a light, but he forced himself to. Kathie had said she had an extra armchair that he could have for his apartment. He really could use that. His wicker computer bench had collapsed under his own weight a few days before as he reacted to one of Simone's more athletic performances. And he was sure Kathie would help him carry the new chair in. That would be the first time she would see his apartment. He turned on another light and realized what a pathetic mess it was compared to Kathie's elegant place. He decided right then to try to figure out the rat's nest of wires that was sprawled across his floor. But the light was still so dim in his apartment he couldn't differentiate all those black cables running across his floor. He thought maybe a slug of cognac would loosen him up so he could get down on the floor and take a closer look. He woke up at three in the morning with a fairly accurate map of the cables impressed on his face.

*** ***

"Don't you understand? I'm not Rhys's boss. He's Building Management. I thought I explained this to you before, Mr. Mallory."

"Look, Harrison. He's given everybody else in her unit a new computer. She's the only one in the company who's supposed to get one who didn't get one. And now he's put another person in her cubicle with her. There's barely enough room in there for either of them to fart." This last word elicited a snort from Peggy, who was still required to record every word of every conversation between Mallory and his manager. "The solution seems pretty simple to me. You have to talk to Rhys. Just tell him how bad she needs this."

"You think I haven't talked to him already? He gave me that same supply-chain bullshit. That fucking asshole's not going to do anything." Peggy raised her eyebrows, caught his eye. "No, Peggy, don't write that down. Oh, go ahead, write down everything. Write down I said he is a fucking asshole."

"Kathie can't do her job while sharing a computer and a cubicle with Meredith. She's a good employee. Remember how she filled in for Chub when he had to go to California to get his daughter back?"

"You know I have nothing against her. She's a great employee."

"Then go higher and complain to the regional manager. What's this big, fat, hierarchal system for if you can't use it to solve serious workplace problems." Mallory was shocked to find himself invoking such platitudes as "workplace problems" and "hierarchal system." He worried that he was losing his touch. But he was constrained from using his usual lies and threats by Peggy sitting there, writing down his every word.

"Peggy, you can go now." Harrison was apparently just as incapable as he was at solving problems with managerial platitudes. Peggy shrugged, screwed up her lips, taking her time getting out of the room as if she had just started enjoying the show.

"Let's be frank, Mr. Mallory. I want to help Kathie. I really do. But you know the position I'm in. You're the one who filed that phony harassment complaint for Ms. Marcie. You might think it was all cleared up, but corporate never forgets. Thanks to you, we have a reputation for chaos here. One more big brouhaha coming out of this branch and we'll all be out the door with the thousands of other employees being laid off due to the Everdine takeover. I know that Rhys is doing Kathie wrong, but I can't do anything about it.

I simply can't go to the regional manager with another personnel problem right now. I can't. And it's all your fault. You wrote that stupid complaint that got Corporate involved." Harrison took a few deep breaths. He asked Mallory to close the door, then took a deeper breath. "As a member of management, I probably shouldn't say this, but has Kathie thought about suing the company?"

Harrison's comment brought home to Mallory that he was facing the most aggravating legal issue of his life. He was used to filing lawsuits and complaints that had no merit whatsoever. He would have filed one for Kathie in a minute. And, unlike every other lawsuit and complaint he had ever filed, this one had merit. Rhys was harassing Kathie, and he was doing it because she was an ex-lover who had thrown him over. Mallory always made a point of never doing any actual research, but he knew in his gut that this one was a winner. But Kathie wouldn't let him file a lawsuit.

"I'll file a complaint with the regional manager myself." Mallory was bluffing, because Kathie had already told him he couldn't do that either.

"You have no credibility with Corporate anymore after that phony complaint you filed for Ms. Marcie."

"I don't care. They need to know what kind of sleaze they have running Building Management."

Harrison slapped his hands flat down on his desk like he was trying to keep it from flying away, then flopped back in his chair and put his hands to his face. "No. No. I'm entreating you, Mr. Mallory." He looked embarrassed for begging for a favor from one of his worst employees, but he went on anyway. "Find me some way I can fix Kathie's problem without involving Corporate. Please."

Chapter 4: Minus Four

Mallory gave Spike full rein to say anything he wanted about Nell. But Spike surprised him. "It's getting old, that lesbian-cat stuff. Less than five hundred new likes today."

"Oh. So, the whole thing's over?"

"No. I told you I have a friend. He set up a completely new website for us! And we created this great cartoon avatar who exemplifies everything we believe in. Look." He shoved his phone in Mallory's face. Mallory saw a caricature of himself, a chubby little guy with red hair and sporting a goatee with beads. He was flying around the screen, making faces, wiggling shamelessly, farting a trail of anti-WOKE sayings in dialogue balloons that floated up and off the screen.

"Flying like a bat out of hell!" Spike was excited. "I'm calling him Mad Mallory. I guarantee people will love him. Mad Mallory's going to rejuvenate the story of the lesbian-cat conspiracy, too. And with him, we can branch out into some of this cultural shit that's going down."

"Doesn't *The Real Honest to God's Truth* already deal with that crap?"

"You don't understand. *God's Truth* is just the source. We have to spread the word, using all our media skills to *popularize* the truths we know. Mad Mallory's the key. And if we get enough hits, we can monetize it."

"What's *monetize*?"

"We can make money off it."

"Oh. Okay. Gotcha."

"And to get more popular, we've got to get sexier, and more political."

"I don't know anything about politics."

"You're making the same mistake everyday Americans are

making. The truth is, you *do* know all you need to know. And all you need to know is in *God's Truth*."

When they started getting over ten thousand total likes a day, Mallory figured Spike must know what he was doing. Spike told him that the re-tweets and re-posts could multiply that figure by the hundreds, if not the thousands. He said that Mad Mallory was on the verge of catching on as a flamboyant and controversial figure, an avatar of frustration and pent-up anger. He said that Mallory should start his own political website. "Once you do, you'll have to post at least three times a day."

"What!"

"Don't worry. I'll take care of everything."

Mallory noticed that Spike was starting to look stressed. His skin was pasty, and he had a tired, haggard look as he slid into the booth and interrupted Mallory's meals every night, staring at him while his eyes glowed in the reflection from the neon sign outside, expostulating about the world gone wrong as Mallory tried to eat his dinner. He was glad when Spike bought another phone to use to pretend he was Mallory. Mallory didn't get too many calls on his real phone, but he wanted to be available in case Kathie might want to reach him someday.

*** ***

Lilly was the sister of Chub, one of Mallory's few friends at UniCast. He had been smitten with her from the instant he first saw her picture on Chub's desk. He had degraded himself entirely and insulted her family in his crude attempt to get her into his bed. Instead of filing any sort of complaint, however, she had been moved by his pathetic lifestyle and had convinced him to attend therapy. But she called him now only when she was arranging to take him there.

Their plan had been for him to start sexual addiction therapy, but he had gone in the wrong door in the church basement and had accidentally joined the Healing Hearts Therapy Group instead. But even after he discovered the error, he had opted to stay with Healing Hearts. He had stayed with it for quite a few sessions, and Lilly had driven him there every week since his Escalade had been repossessed. She was twenty-five, and hot, but she was working on her master's degree in accounting and was running Roofs, a non-profit housing agency – definitely different from the kind of women he used to read about every night on his *Manly Man* website.

"Still living alone?" he asked her now.

"Yeah. Still in my new apartment. It seems like I'm hardly ever there, though, what with my new position at Roofs, and graduate courses at night. And helping Chub keep an eye on little Stephanie."

Mallory suspected she was avoiding the obvious point of his question. He was starting to realize women did that sometimes. He wanted to get to that point. "Aren't you making it with Officer Selby now?"

Mallory was proud to see her embarrassed look. He relished having at least that much power over this bright young businesswoman looking so pretty with her hair dramatically upswept into in a dark French twist. He felt she owed him information. After all, he was the one who originally got her together with that friendly neighborhood cop.

"You know that's none of your business, Kevin."

"Tell me this much. Is he living there?"

She focused her eyes on the road as if she were moving into a complicated driving situation. She took a breath, then halfway smiled as if she were just a little pleased that he cared. She was seven years younger than he was, but she treated him sometimes like a lost little brother she had to be honest with. "Okay. We're not living together. We talk on the phone sometimes, that's all."

"What a waste."

She ignored his comment as she pulled her car to a stop in the church parking lot.

After she drove away, he paused at the top of the concrete steps leading to the church basement. He had begun therapy just so he could keep in touch with her. But then he had made a tragic mistake. Once he had introduced her in the church parking lot to his police officer friend, Selby, he rarely saw either of them again. And Selby had been not only his friend but also his hero. In retrospect, it made perfect sense for this splendid woman and this hero officer to fall in love, but he hadn't anticipated that. In the last year, Mallory had made the first few friends of his entire adult life. Now, two of them were basically paired off, leaving little time for him. It didn't seem fair. He had hooked up his two friends, and now he was minus two.

Mallory was relieved to see that Grace was at the meeting. She was already seated, and she motioned with her head toward the chair next to her. Her short, blonde hair was more stylishly cut now. Grace had bonded with Mallory after her mother died. She had described to the group how devastated she was by that loss, but he was the only one from the therapy group who came to the funeral. Over time, he had confessed to her some of his flaws, but she still seemed to think he was sort of normal. Their connection wasn't anything romantic. He could accept that. What bothered him was that she did make a romantic connection with Thomas, Mallory's only other male friend besides Selby. Mallory had introduced the two, and now he didn't see much of either of them anymore. Altogether, between Lilly and Selby and Grace and Thomas, he had helped hook up four friends in the past year, and now he was minus four.

Mallory was having a hard time concentrating on the therapeutic mumbo-jumbo. He was thinking instead about Kathie. She kept telling him that he would never get anywhere unless he made more money. He thought that was maybe true. He was no longer cutting a dashing figure in his suit or making an impression on the streets with his Escalade. He couldn't take a woman anywhere that cost money, or even buy more cognac for his apartment.

He needed a promotion at the very least. Harrison, of course, would never support anything like that. And UniCast was using every excuse to get rid of people, not promote them. But Harrison himself was vulnerable after the Miss Marcie affair. UniCast would now be glad to get rid of Harrison. All they needed was one more incident.

Chapter 5: Mad Mallory and the Nell Chronicles

"You're big! You're big! Mad Mallory is trending everywhere." Mallory noticed that Spike seemed to have regained some of his natural color as he slid down onto the bench across from him in his booth at the Dough and Go.

"What things am I saying?"

"The truth. Nothing but the *God's Truth*." Spike smiled at his own reference to their favorite website.

"I'm not sure I want to keep doing this. How much is it costing to pay that Mad Mallory artist, and to use that extra phone?"

"Don't you realize? That's the beauty of this. If we go much over ten thousand followers, we can start to collect money from advertisers."

"Money? Really?"

Mallory had been thinking about money for a few days. Kathie was encouraging him to take a job she said was available at a car dealership. "I found it on the internet. It's just a part-time, evening job."

"I don't know anything about cars," he had told her then.

"The job is as a Service Advisor. That's pretty much like customer assistance, I think. Kind of like what you're doing for UniCast Cable already."

He couldn't bear to tell her how much he hated working in customer assistance. "I don't know what I would say. I don't know anything about cars."

"I think you just talk to the customers, tell them what's wrong with their cars, how much it's going to cost, when it's ready. Stuff like that."

"How would I know what's wrong with their cars?"

"You don't have to know any of that stuff. The mechanics, or whoever knows that kind of stuff, tells you. You just pass the information on to the customers."

"I'll think about it."

"Honestly, Kevin, you need to do something. It was great of you to pay with your credit card for all the damage the Cheer Committee did to the Pirate Bar, but you really didn't have that kind of money. Then you leased that Escalade you couldn't afford. Then you bought those fancy suits that you don't wear anymore. Now you're in a financial hole. You're dressing worse. You're looking worse. And you can't count on me driving you around forever."

Mallory was glad he hadn't gone along with Kathie's idea right away. Spike was telling him now they were almost ready to make money on the internet. Spike told him it was easy to get "content" just by elaborating on the ideas that showed up almost every day on *The Real Honest to God's Truth*. "But it's not just that. It's you, your personality, your Mad Mallory charisma – as I've designed it. You're established on the internet as a unique character, with a unique voice. You're personifying the average man who's been left behind by all this WOKE business. It would be a total waste not to exploit that."

"Yeah, I agree," Mallory said, but that wasn't true. Kathie had told him that a person like Spike, who couldn't even get into business school, was not likely to create a profit-making business based just on a conspiracy blog. Mallory didn't tell her about their additional special ingredient, his charisma. He couldn't bring himself to brag about his charisma to her face. He had the feeling she would laugh. When he was with Spike, though, he nodded along in agreement with everything he said. If Spike was right, Kathie would find out soon enough.

Nell confronted him just outside his cubicle two days after his last talk with Spike. "You said you would stop, but you totally lied to me."

"I don't know what you're talking about."

"Come into my cubicle, you idiot, and I'll show you." Nell then broke all the rules of UniCast Cable by going on the internet from her work desk. Mallory was shocked to see *Mad Mallory to the Rescue* appear in a YouTube video on her screen. He guessed this was the political website Spike had talked about. Nell had figured out that he was Mad Mallory. She must have recognized the beaded goatee similar to the one he used to flaunt. That didn't make him feel any better. Nell clicked on the video. At first, they just saw Mad Mallory twerk his way across the screen. But then he suddenly turned toward the audience and moved closer until his face and goatee filled up the whole screen. He started reciting his screed in an angry, tinny voice. The movements of his mouth didn't exactly sync with the words, but the message was clear enough.

We're going to talk today about an especially poisonous branch of the LGBTQ-plusses community. These are frustrated gay females who cannot even form a relationship with their own kind. They have been known not only to abuse and torture cats, as we have reported before, but they have also been known recently to harass normal heterosexual women co-workers who would not submit to their incessant deviant demands. We call these people Nells.

Nell clicked it off and looked up at him, her glowering face as angry as he had ever seen it. "Your word is no good, Kevin. You are absolute scum."

Mallory realized that Spike was ridiculing Nell for supposedly harassing Kathie, even though Mallory had told him flatly that it wasn't true. But he also remembered that he and Spike were getting close to 75,000 followers on all media combined. He knew now he had been right to buy into Spike's vision. And he kind of enjoyed how Spike was trashing Nell. He thought he'd join in on the fun right here, in person.

"You and Rhys are torturing Kathie. You and Rhys are making her share a cubicle and a computer with that stinky Meredith. Kathie's the only one in that division that didn't get a new computer.

Rhys is doing that, and I know it's all part of your LGBT revenge for her turning straight."

"Who's Rhys?"

"Don't play dumb, Nell. You and Rhys have now found a way to make Kathie's life miserable."

Nell stood up so fast her chair slammed into the cubicle partition behind her. Mallory retreated until he backed himself into the wall across the corridor. He saw her still coming at him, and his legs went weak. He couldn't move. Her angry, clenched face took up his entire field of vision. He closed his eyes and waited for the punishment to come. He could feel the sweat dripping down from his armpits.

But she didn't hit him. He knew she was still there, but only because he could still hear her breathing. He thought he could smell her anger.

"Aren't you going to open your eyes, you coward?"

"No. Go away. Please."

He heard the footsteps of some other workers coming down the corridor. When the sound got close, he dared to open his eyes. Nell had been forced to back up to let them through. He turned to follow them and found himself crossing the lobby and out onto the concrete apron of the building. The group scattered to their cars, but he kept walking until he was all the way across the parking lot and near its entrance to the road. He was afraid to come back, so he missed his ride home with Kathie that day.

*** ***

"It's good to have enemies," Spike explained. "You can't just be spouting philosophy all the time. People get bored of that after a while. They want someone to hate. You've got something going really good with this *Nell* business. It's like your own catchword, and it's catching on."

"She tried to hit me."

"Great! Assault by a *Nell*. We've got a character, and a story, and now we have an enemy. People will eat this up. If you can egg her on, get a video of her hitting you, every damn person on the internet will want to see what a *Nell* looks like in action."

Mallory was not interested in going this route, but he was excited by what Spike said next. "We're getting close to the number of followers we need to attract sponsors. I'm studying, googling all the time to see how we can monetize – you know, make money off it. I'm getting real close to figuring that out."

But Mallory wondered when Spike would be able to deliver on his promises. He started discussing Spike's plans with Kathie as they drove to work every day. He made sure to call them "Spike's plans," rather than his own. Kathie had said a lot of people were trying to make a fortune with some gimmick on the internet, but few succeeded.

A few days later, as he was creeping towards the break room, looking warily into Nell's cubicle as he passed by, he felt someone hit him so hard from his blind side that he was almost knocked to the floor. It was Kathie. He realized only at the last second, as he stumbled backwards into the wall, that it was supposed to be a hug.

"I don't know how you did it, but one of the new computers was on my desk when I got here this morning! You've done it again. You are some kind of deviant genius, Kevin."

He had to catch his breath. He didn't think this kind of harsh contact with a female was appropriate. Especially since she was six inches taller than he was. But as he regained his composure, he tried to figure out if there was a way he could take credit for this fortunate computer event. It didn't make sense. Rhys had been enjoying Kathie's discomfort too much to change plans. Harrison was intimidated from complaining to upper management. Mallory hadn't yet come up with a plan to force Harrison's hand.

"We have to thank Harrison," Kathie insisted now. He followed a few steps behind her, head down.

Ms. Marcie and Peggy tried to stop them from entering Harrison's inner office, but Kathie marched right through their protests, with Mallory following behind. They were surprised to find Harrison on his knees behind his desk. Mallory smiled at the thought of finding his boss in the middle of a seamy sexcapade. Harrison, stunned silent, visibly cringed at the sight of the two of them. There seemed to be someone or something under his desk that he didn't want them to see. Mallory rounded the corner of the desk and leaned forward to catch sight of who it was. But he was surprised that there was no one else under there.

"You're not supposed to be in my office!" Harrison didn't get off his knees.

Kathie brushed off his anger. "For God's sake, we just came to thank you. For getting Rhys to give me that computer. Thank you. We can leave you alone now." She turned to Mallory. "Let's go."

But Mallory studied the scene for a second longer. His mouth dropped open as he met Harrison's eyes. "Wait. Where's *your* computer?"

Harrison crawled back out from a tangle of cables under his desk and slowly climbed back into his chair. "I don't have a computer right now. I came in early this morning and gave mine to Kathie. New cables and all. I can get my old one back."

"What?" Kathie's voice was too loud.

"Shhh. I had to do it. It's not that I'm that good of a guy. Mr. Mallory had me trapped. I had no other way out. Now get out of my office. And don't tell Ms. Marcie."

Chapter 6: Breaking the Pattern

Mallory was disappointed that Kathie was leaving her high-rise apartment with that distant view of the lake and moving to a smaller, one-bedroom, fourth floor apartment. But he hoped that the move would obliterate any last vestiges of her memory of her time with Rhys. She had hired movers for all the furniture and most of the boxes. She said all Mallory had to do was carry small boxes and loose things from her current high rise to her truck, then to the new, not-quite-so-high rise. But there were probably twenty or thirty small boxes. She said they were full of fragile stuff and insisted they each carry only one at a time. It soon became apparent that she had underestimated the job. After ten or fifteen trips back and forth, up and down, in and out of the chilled buildings and then into the warm September weather, Mallory was covered in sweat and totally out of breath. He had not worked that hard in years.

"Thanks, Kevin. I'm sorry. I didn't realize there were so many boxes." But after that breath of apology, she went on. "Now, let's now sort them all and get each of them in its right place, in the right room."

Still breathing heavily, he cut his eyes over to her. He had a sinking feeling that he was repeating a depressing scenario from his past. It seemed like he was doing a project like those he had often done for his mother, moving her furniture and knickknacks around as the mood struck her, arranging each piece as she directed, then moving it again as she changed her mind, then moving it again. And again. Everything always had to be exactly as she wanted, even in the basement bedroom where he had moved in a futile attempt to escape her constant criticism. And she was always changing her mind about how it was to be done. It was almost as if she wanted to keep him constantly on the run. Now he was jolted to see the same pattern starting up in his relationship with Kathie.

His heart sank. He just could not repeat this pattern, not even for this fantastic woman.

"No."

She shivered like she had been given a tiny shock, then seemed to shake it off. "Oh. I'm sorry. You've done enough. You look beat. Forget that. I'm so used to bossing people around …. Here, relax. And thanks so much. And I owe you a beer." She waved him toward a sofa that the movers had dumped in the middle of the living room in her new place. She sat down next to him. She seemed to be getting used to him.

And now she was apologizing. "I have this kind of fear of clutter. I think it comes from living with Rhys. I felt like, *ick,* every time I walked in the door."

"Is that why you broke up with him?"

"No, that's another story. A long story. I don't want to get into that now."

She looked exhausted. She had new tangles in her hair. She crossed her legs in those light blue jeans, jiggling her dangling white running shoes. Too tired to talk, they each sipped their beers in almost complete silence. Kathie sighed and met his eyes. Her curls were drooping a little. Her T-shirt was dirty, she looked tired. Mallory liked her just as much this way as when she was dressed to kill. In fact, she was a little less intimidating this way.

He had to catch his breath as she changed position. He hoped she was going to lean into him and let him put his arm around her. No such luck. He had never cracked that kind of romantic code with her. He knew she could be wildly sexual. He had seen that with his own eyes. And she was much prettier than Simone, his nighttime porn queen. He sometimes tried to imagine it was Kathie's screams coming from the computer screen, but that always made his loneliness worse.

"You know," she said lazily, "I think I'm going to lie down and take a nap."

He couldn't stop his manly powers from jerking awake. He

found himself waiting for an invitation, but she didn't say or do anything more. "I'm tired, too," was all he could think of to say.

"I mean, I'll drive you home. Then I'm taking a nap."

"Oh." His voice came out weak, but he was so disheartened he didn't care how he sounded.

"What's wrong?"

His exhaustion worked like truth serum. He forgot to be afraid. He asked her the question he had never asked of her – or of anyone – before. "What do you think of me, really?"

She stared at him, her mouth hanging open like this was the hardest question in the world. She broke eye contact. "I'm still amazed at your knack for keeping UniCast honest. For us employees, I mean."

He already knew she thought that. He had recognized that amazed look on her face when Harrison had crawled out from under his desk. But she seemed to be afraid to answer his real question. He had just enough courage left for one more try. "But will you ever go out with me?"

"You can't afford to go out with anybody."

He was dying to tell her that he and Spike now had thousands of followers, but he knew that would mean nothing to her.

"Okay. So, if I ditch the internet crap, and get a real second job, and get myself out of debt, would you date me then?"

"I'd like to see if you can do that."

Chapter 7: The $99 Mushroom

Spike seemed aggravated that Mallory had missed the previous Saturday evening at the Dough and Go.

"Where were you, man? We're going totally viral now. We have the chance to make real progress, real money, but you have to keep up. Where were you?" Mallory didn't want to tell him that he spent the whole day helping Kathie move. Fortunately, Spike was too excited to stay irritated for long. "Mad Mallory has singlehandedly made a star out of Simone de Boudoir! Her site got so many hits it totally crashed! She had to set up a new site."

"You're saying *I* did this?"

"Well, of course, *I'm* the one who really did it. You told me she's the one who turns you on. I had a feeling that *The Real Honest to God's Truth* was too highbrow for a lot of people. So I started hyping her at the end of each of your posts. Little screen shots, man. And I put comments underneath. Funny comments. And I added a link to her website. That's all it took. It crashed. She had to set up a new website. And now she's a star. She's charging $99 a month now! People loved your off-beat comments."

Mallory had never thought there was anything funny about Simone. Her siren call usually came to him late at night, when he was tired but couldn't sleep, when hour after hour crept slowly toward dawn, when he knew the next day of his life would move at the same petty pace, without anything changing. Those were the desperate hours when his urge to live life large was reduced to what he could pull up on his 36-inch computer screen.

But Spike was certainly excited. "Don't you want to see Mad Mallory's funny comments about Simone? And the responses you're getting?"

"$99 a month? I won't get to see her at all anymore."

"Yes you will! You're sure to go viral yourself soon. The money will come pouring in."

"I would like my food now."

Kathie had been telling him that his constant diet of burgers, fries and cinnamon buns was probably not very good for his health, so he ordered just a cheese steak sub and a side of apple pie instead. Spike stood up quickly to start working on his order. He seemed miffed that Mallory wasn't more enthused about his manufactured internet fame.

Mallory didn't believe that Spike was right about the money. He knew he was not the kind of person who could magically strike it rich like that. He wasn't one of the fortunate ones making billions while living off the people doing the hard work at the bottom of the economic pyramid. He himself had never received a penny from anyone except in exchange for pretending to do hard work. And those pennies didn't add up to much. Now he wouldn't be able to afford Simone anymore. He didn't know if he could forgive Spike for that.

*** ***

Mallory began to obsess about Kathie's affair with Rhys. He came up with the idea of asking her how long they had been together, or what attracted her to him in the first place, or why they broke up. He was thinking he might learn something about her that way so he could copy the parts of Rhys she liked. But he certainly couldn't copy Rhys's lean, strong body, chiseled face, or piercing dark eyes. And he was tired, and he didn't have the energy to start up any such long-term plan. He decided that for now he'd go with Manly Man's typical advice and strike while the iron was hot.

"Will you come into my apartment tonight?" he asked her on the way to work the next day.

"Are you going to make me dinner?" But then she smiled at the alarmed look on his face. "Just kidding. I don't think I could eat anything you could make. But I could use a drink."

"I have some leftover cognac…and water, if that's what you want."

She went to his apartment that evening on the way back from work, but she just took water. "I'll let you save your cognac. I know you can't afford to buy any more." He wanted a drink so badly he went into the kitchen and brought back a small glass of cognac for himself.

"I need to say something to you," she started. "Apologize, really." She had his attention. He put down his glass. "Back when I was going out with Nell for all those girls' nights out on Fridays, when you were stuck babysitting her three cats and two dogs, I had absolutely no idea that you were interested in her. I would never have gone out with her at all if I knew you cared about her. Really, I thought Nell and I were just friends, and I thought you just liked taking care of animals and were making a little money on the side."

"She didn't pay me."

"Oh. That's worse. I'm sorry."

"It's okay."

"But I want to say something more. This is a confession. There was one night when Nell and I – you know, *did the deed*. I was just feeling lonely, and I was drunk. But it was just that one night. I admit I was excited that one night. But I don't think that's really who I am. But now that I totally broke it off with Nell, and she told everybody, everybody at work, men and women, they all look at me funny. I mean, it's like half of them think I would fuck anybody, and the other half wouldn't touch me with a ten-foot pole. I so much wish it had never happened."

Mallory had no idea what to say. "So, you spread a little love a little too far over the line. Nobody can blame you for that."

She met his eyes. "Thanks. Really. Just you saying that makes me feel a little bit better."

Just her saying *that* made *him* feel a *lot* better. He hadn't done

Mallory Meets His Match

anything but listen to her story, a story that he had pretty much known already.

"Thanks for listening," she said. "What about you, Mr. Mallory?" She suddenly jerked forward in her chair. "Wait. I know what's up with you. You need a job, Kevin, to get you out of your financial hole. Let's look up that job at Lou's Lexus right now."

She rushed over to the computer bench and clicked it on and demanded his password. She clicked right in before he could even think. "Hey, what does RHGT mean?"

"That's the bookmark for *The Real Honest to God's Truth*." Mallory thought he might as well let her look. If they were going to get to know each other, she would eventually need to find out what his core beliefs were. He was not going to seduce her today, but maybe he could make some progress on introducing her to his inner soul. "Click on it," he said.

He had second thoughts when she opened the introductory page, where RHGT set out its Ten Commandments. She started reading them out loud. "One: There is only one God, and only God's Martyrs can see His truth. Two: It is every Martyr's duty to fight the forces that are undermining our values and our sacred traditions. Three: The only pure model of family life …." She clicked it off. "This is boring."

Mallory was glad she didn't get to Four, Five and Six. But a surge of panic ran through him when she quickly clicked on his second bookmark, his "Friends" bookmark, which was his code for Simone de Boudoir. "Oh my God," she said when it opened, though he imagined her tone was more curious than disgusted. "This is your love life?" she chuckled. "Oh well, I guess a lot of men look at this kind of stuff. Let's see what's on the next bookmark. What's this one called 'Self-help' about?"

"No!"

With a lot of help from Spike, Mallory had recently been trying to make use of the camera and the split screen on his computer. He had used this technical knowledge to bring up Simone on one

49

screen while recording – in an artistic way, of course – his manly reactions to her on the other screen. His plan had been to send the second screen to his girlfriend – if he ever got a girlfriend. But he now feared Kathie would run screaming out of his apartment like Lilly had done once before. But she surprised him again.

"Oh, this is interesting."

"You think it's *interesting*?" That word wasn't even close to any of the words he had expected.

"Oh, yeah. This is one of those foraging shows, right? I like this kind of thing. Oh, what's that? A toadstool?"

"Um … yes. A toadstool." His voice was shaky, but his hand was quick to reach around her and click off the screen. "Let's go to the Lou's Lexus website now."

Chapter 8: A Suitable Employee

"You have reached UniCast Cable's Customer Assistance line. All of our assistants are busy right now, but if you take a number someone will call you back some time after the first full moon of April."

"Kevin, cut it out. This is Kathie. I just called Lou's Lexus this morning. What they said on their website was true. It sounds like they really need a Service Advisor."

"I can't fix cars."

"I told you. It's not about fixing cars. I mean, it's sort of about fixing cars, but you wouldn't have to fix them yourself, or know anything about fixing them."

"I like my job here."

"Listen. The job at Lou's is a part-time, evening job. I know you need the money. Everybody knows you're broke. The job starts at five, so you'd have a half-hour to get there from here."

"I don't have a car."

"I told you. I'll drive you there, at least for a while. After that you'd have to get your own car."

A sudden swelling of sadness threw him off track. "But if I get my own car, you won't drive me to work every day."

"Don't be silly. We can carpool."

Mallory could produce only one good reference from all his twelve previous jobs. The reference was in praise of his three-week stint as a barista several years ago. That good reference was part of a settlement of a lawsuit Mallory had filed after his manager had hit him on the side of his head, supposedly accidentally, in the middle of a melee between Mallory and an enraged customer. Kathie told him that one reference from a place where he worked for three weeks, ten years ago, wouldn't help him much, so Mallory worked hard on his application to buff up his image. Kathie drove him to his interview with Rick Gunther, the service manager of Lou's Lexus. Rick stood up from behind his desk when Mallory approached. He was a massive man with a fake smile that showed two rows of oversized teeth. He didn't look like he belonged behind a desk, and in fact his desktop was almost entirely empty. Even with his receding hairline and the beginnings of a paunch, he looked like someone Mallory would not want to get into an argument with.

"So, you want to be a service writer for us here at Lou's Lexus."

"Yes sir, that's why I'm here."

"You know what the pay is?"

"Um, sixteen dollars an hour?"

"Sit down, son. Right. Sixteen, but that's just the bottom line."

"I understand." He didn't understand.

"Let me explain how this works. The service writer is the go-between. The mechanics tell you what's wrong with the car, you tell the customers. The mechanics tell you when it's finished. You tell the customers when it's done and what the bill is."

"I have a lot of experience dealing with customers and their problems."

"Good. But I'm talking about the money. On top of the base salary, the service writer also gets a commission on every sale. One percent on every paid repair charge. I'm telling you, we've had service writers who double their base salary with these commissions."

That sounded good to Mallory. What didn't sound good was that he'd have to see his customers in person. But he was determined to get the job, to get out of debt, to prove to Kathie he was the kind of man she wanted. He hoped that the interview was over. He felt he had done well so far. But then he saw Rick bring up his application on the computer screen.

"It says here you drove in the Escalade 500. I don't think I've ever heard of that race." Rick managed a sour look with slightly raised eyebrows. Mallory could feel the interview going south already. He didn't know why he had made up that fact, but he knew now he had to keep going. He nodded vaguely. But Rick wouldn't let it go.

"I've been following the NASCAR and Grand Prix races for thirty years, but I've never heard of the Escalade 500." The service manager leveled his eyes at him.

"It's a new thing," Mallory offered. When the manager didn't let him get away with just that, he added. "It only started up a couple of years ago."

"That's funny. I think I would have heard of that. Where does it take place?"

Mallory had not anticipated hard questions like this. Kathie had told him they were desperate for a warm body to answer the telephones after 5:00 p.m. when customers called to see if their cars were fixed. He was happy enough that Kathie considered him a warm body. But it seemed from this interview that there was much more to the job. He now had to come up with an imaginary location for this imaginary race. He didn't know, but it seemed like any race called a "500" would have to take place in a pretty big state.

"Alaska."

"So, this Escalade 500 is run in Alaska. What time of year does it run?"

Mallory recognized the manager's trick question. "Summer, of course. There's too much snow in Alaska in the winter."

"Oh. But I've never heard of any tracks in Alaska that could handle a 500."

"They run it in parts. Part on the regular roads, part on the track – on and off several tracks, actually."

"How do you handle pit stops, then?"

"Um. There aren't any pit stops. There are no gas stations in Alaska anyway." Mallory then saw a chance for a little more embellishment. "You have to carry your own gas in cans inside the car. Those Escalades are really big inside."

"I see. Is this some new kind of stock car race?"

"Um, yeah. They have stocks and stocks of cars."

"I see." Gunther nodded thoughtfully. "Did you win?"

Mallory recognized another trick question. "I came in second

53

– I didn't get any trophy or anything. But that was just because the other guy cheated."

"Oh, what a shame. What was your time?"

"Um, they don't have times. It's just, like, if you finish or not."

Rick Gunther leaned forward and slapped his huge forearms on the desk so suddenly that Mallory jerked back in his chair. "Mr. Mallory, I've been in this business a long time, and I think I know a complete bullshitter when I see one." Mallory jumped up, knocking his chair down behind him, but before he could turn to run, Gunther reached up with a giant hand and grabbed him by the wrist. "I think you're just the kind of guy we need here at Lou's Lexus."

"Um. You really think I can do it?"

"You're a natural. You'll fit right in in my service department. Welcome to the team."

*** ***

Spike was furious when Mallory told him that night that he wouldn't be coming to the Dough and Go for dinner on weeknights.

"Just when we're starting to really move, you're quitting on me?"

"I'm not quitting on you." Mallory didn't really understand Spike's accusation. He didn't understand how he could quit when he had hardly done anything at all. "Why do you need me, anyway?"

"We're just about to cash in on this *Mad Mallory* business. Thanks to Mad Mallory, we have over 25,000 followers on our X account alone. And X is going to pay us! A cat food supplement company, Cat-A-Tonic, has just agreed to pay for each mention in our tweets for the next ten days. That's because every cat lover in the country will soon be following us. Here, I'll give you your cut right now." Spike quickly stepped over to the cash register and pulled out some bills. "Here, 150 for you. This is only the beginning. You're welcome."

Mallory was thrilled. He promised he would keep up his end of the business, even if he could only come in every Saturday.

"Good. That money is nothing. Longer-term advertising deals are pending. If we hit 100,000 on X – and I'm sure we will soon, what with the *Nell* thing trending – X will pay us real money! And there's a group in Dallas that claims they can help us get possibly a million followers, and they have connections with politicians who will pay thousands for mentions in our posts, but only if we keep growing."

"Sounds great." Mallory really was interested now. It seemed like he would be wasting his time at Lou's Lexus at sixteen dollars an hour if thousands were pouring in based on Spike's posts while he did nothing at all. If Spike was right, he could afford as many Simones as he wanted, even at $99 a month. "What'll I have to do?"

"Nothing! You're doing great. You're trending!" Spike's eyes were lit up now. "It's okay. We can talk here on Saturdays. That's all the meetings we really need."

Mallory thought things couldn't be working out any better. Spike was making him rich while Kathie was admiring him for taking the job at Lou's. He was a little sorry that *Nell* was becoming the new, preferred term for lesbian animal torturer, but he put that out of his mind. Aside from the *Nell* business, he had no idea what Spike was doing, and he was sure that he would never be able to understand it. And Spike had said he didn't need to do a single thing to help.

"Oh, there's one thing you might have to do," Spike quickly corrected himself. "There are some people who want to meet us. Rich people. Potential sponsors. We might have to fly out to Dallas, stay in a hotel one night. But they'll pay for everything. That's how much they want us!"

Chapter 9: No Pent-Up Anger

Mallory and Kathie had just finished the complete cleaning and rearranging of Mallory's tiny efficiency apartment. Kathie had given him her small, beige, upholstered chair, and they had found a computer bench at a yard sale that looked like it would hold Mallory's weight. Once the furniture was in, the whole project hadn't taken more than another hour. But Kathie refused to clean, or even go into, his bathroom.

She agreed to break in his new décor with a double shot of cognac for each of them. She sat on the sofa while he occupied the beige chair. As much as he enjoyed working with her, he didn't seem to be getting any closer to winning her heart – or her anything else. And he found himself struggling now just to think of anything to say.

"Do you miss your friends from the Cheer Committee at work?"

She looked up as if surprised he had talked about anything but himself. "A little. I told you Valerie and Gretchen ghosted me. They blame me for breaking Nell's heart. You know, that's one of those situations – how can I explain what happened without hurting *somebody's* feelings. So, I've had to kind of give up on having work friends, except for you and Chub."

"You don't have any friends?"

"I have friends. I'm still friends with Chub's sister, Lilly. And I have girlfriends outside of work. We go out a lot." She waited, as if doubting he wanted to hear any more about her friends. But he surprised her by waiting, listening for her to go on. "I have this idea about friends. In the end, your family, mainly your brothers and your sisters, they are the ones who will really stick by you. They're your deepest friends, you might say. I didn't believe that until recently. But don't you think that's true?"

"I don't have any brothers or sisters."

"Oh, I'm sorry. Maybe my theory applies only to me. I'm sure it's not just brothers and sisters that will stick by you."

"I guess so." But he didn't have anything else to say, and that seemed to end the conversation. Mallory didn't feel he had gotten anywhere with her. He took a big last gulp of his cognac.

"But, Kevin, thanks for listening to me." She drained the last of her drink, then looked up brightly. "And I just have to tell you one more thing. My brother and sister and I all live in different states. For years, we saw each other maybe twice a year. But last summer, the three of us planned a family reunion in Mexico at a place called the Riviera Maya. I was having a really hard time then. I'd just discovered some awful, personal thing. I was crying all the way on the plane, wondering if I should tell them, if I could tell them."

She checked to see if he was still listening. "But, Kevin, they just *knew*. We all grew up together, and when they saw me, they just *knew*. I've never felt so not-alone before. There was a lot of crying at first, but then it sort of melted away and we did everything you could possibly do in that town, and it was *magical*, and the magic had nothing to do with the tourist things themselves."

Mallory was trying hard to understand her story. He could tell that it was important to her, but he had no idea what to say. She quickly stood up and mumbled sheepishly that she had to leave. On her way out the door, though, she suddenly turned around, leaned down and hugged him tight for just a second.

"Wha ...?"

"Oh. Sorry." She seemed as startled as he was. "I'd better get going." And she was out the door before Mallory had a chance to say anything. Not that he had any idea what to say.

She was not like any of the women he had ever dated. She was hardworking and honest to a fault, but she hadn't hesitated to stretch the statistics so he would look better at the job than he really was. And she told him she did that because she thought he was worth it to the employees, no matter how badly UniCast might otherwise judge his performance. And she drove him to work every day. And she got him a job. And she helped him straighten up his apartment. And she told him a mysterious story about something that had really made her sad. And she hugged him.

After she left, he sat down on his new beige chair. He wondered how often she had sat in it. It fit him just right, so he imagined her legs had hung out over the edge of the cushion a little bit. He wondered who else had sat in it. He wondered if she and Rhys had sat in it together. Kathie had also told him she used to date someone who worked at Lou's. But he decided it was a mistake to think about who had been in that chair. After all, he was the one sitting in it now.

Throughout his adult life, Mallory's core belief had been that when a man and a woman were in a room together and the passion between them was rising, nothing but that instant in time had any meaning whatsoever. But now, even after Kathie's hug had implanted wild ideas in his mind, he felt that being in that room with her in that instant in time was not all that he wanted. But he wasn't sure what else it was he wanted.

He guessed that showing up for his new job at Lou's might keep him going with Kathie. He didn't think the job itself would be hard. He didn't know anything about cars, but he was used to faking it. Talking to the other workers at the dealership would be hard, though, because every time he dealt with anyone at Lou's, he'd be wondering if that was the one who had once sat in that beige chair. He wished Kathie would tell him every detail of her affair with every guy. Usually, this was something he didn't want to know. It was easier to imagine women had been waiting all their lives for him. But part of Kathie's attraction for him was the undeniable fact that she had been living a fascinating life for years before they even met.

His other friend, Lilly, drove him to therapy again that week. By the time he started to explain to her his own confusion about Kathie, they were pulling into the church parking lot. Lilly said she was in a hurry and suggested, very kindly but firmly, that maybe the therapy group was exactly the place where he could talk out his problem and get some advice.

Mallory Meets His Match

He trudged down the stairs into the church basement. He often told himself that his problems were too unique, and ran too deep, to be solved by this bunch of losers, but the truth was he had made a friend there, Grace. And Sebastian, the facilitator, seemed competent and kind. Sebastian had gradually led him over the past few weeks to the realization that he didn't always have to act out the role of the arrogant but cowardly bully that his father had assigned to him years ago. And the other members of the group were coming around. They didn't act as appalled now at everything he said. He had spent most of his adult life on the defensive, but he was beginning to relax here. The other group members had gradually elicited his confession to the damage he had done to himself and to everyone around him, but they still seemed to think he could be cured. But when he looked up at Sebastian now, he suspected he was being betrayed.

"Excuse me. Before we start, I have an announcement. We have today a new member of our Healing Hearts Therapy Group." Sebastian projected his own quiet, non-judgmental persona every time he spoke to the group. He turned and gestured for the woman standing behind him to step forward. "Please give a warm welcome to our newest member, Ms. Nell Pickens."

Mallory found the courage to protest. "This woman hates me! She's just coming here to ruin the one thing that I have going that makes any sense to me." He turned to Sebastian, pleaded. "You just can't let her in."

"Well, now," Sebastian began with his usual, preternatural calmness. "Like everyone else who has ever come to this group, Ms. Pickens has expressed a desire to work on her personal issues."

"That lezzie bitch just wants to trash me!" Mallory shouted. He found himself standing up on shaking legs. He'd never confronted anybody like this in public before. Grace, sitting next to him, put her hand on his arm and gently pulled him down. "Excuse me. I didn't mean to yell," he found himself mumbling. He didn't know why he was being even that polite.

Nell smirked when she saw Grace touch Mallory.

Sebastian turned to Nell. "You don't have to defend your right to be here, miss. We at Healing Hearts welcome all who feel the need to discuss their issues. Mr. Ramsteel, if there are issues between the two of you, it might be of help to both of you to discuss them in this neutral, safe space."

Grace turned to Mallory and whispered in his ear. "Just do it. Talk to her. How bad can it be?"

"Who's Mr. Ramsteel?" Nell looked puzzled.

"We'll explain that later," Sebastian seemed like he didn't want any more distractions. "Let's get on with the meeting." Mallory kept quiet.

Sebastian had all the other members of the group introduce themselves. Nell introduced herself as a co-worker of Mallory – "Ramsteel," Sebastian had to explain. Then she told the group in a rush that Mallory had repeatedly lied to her, gotten her drunk, tried to seduce her by trickery, invented a fictitious friend to cover his lies, made her falsely confess publicly to committing exotic lesbian abuse on her cat, stolen the cat, turned her one true love against her, and was now conducting a constant internet campaign against her personally – "to the point where I might have to change my name."

The group went silent.

"Well, we certainly have a lot of issues to unpack," Sebastian spoke into the silence. "Let me start with this observation. Ms. Pickens, I don't think you would have come all the way here to accuse Mr. Ramsteel if you hadn't had in the past at least some kind of expectation of a better relationship with him."

"No. That's a lie." Nell's rash reply got the attention of the whole group.

"That was just a suggestion. But can you tell us why it matters to you that we all know about the injuries Mr. Ramsteel has inflicted on you in the past?"

"Because I don't want you to fall for all his lies."

"It's true, Ms. Pickens. We're not the FBI. We don't check out the truth about everything anybody says in this room. But the only person who is hurt by lying in a group like this is the group member who is not being honest about himself."

"What about that girl over there?" Nell pointed at Grace. "She's fawning all over him. If she knew the truth about him …."

Grace stood up, suddenly breathing hard, and took a step toward Nell. "How dare you! Mr. Ramsteel has been very kind to me. He's not hitting on me. In fact, he introduced me to my current boyfriend."

"Let's everyone take a moment!" Sebastian's voice was shockingly commanding, as if he were desperate to get back in control of the group. But he seemed to relax once Grace sat back down. "Here's what I want us to do. This group is not the place to argue about who has done worse to whom in the past. The best we can do is have an honest exchange about our current feelings. Mr. Ramsteel and Ms. Pickens, I would like you both to discuss your relationship with the group so we can maybe uncover the deeper feelings behind your history of contention."

"My only deeper feeling is he should go to jail." Nell's sour grimace looked very familiar to Mallory.

Mallory sensed that Sebastian's instructions were to his advantage. He quickly jumped into the conversation. He focused on the fact that he had been deeply in love with Nell. All she could say in response was she was never in love with him. All her accusations about kidnapped cats and fictitious friends and attempted seductions and missing panties and stealing away her ex-lover were made to seem trivial compared to Mallory's heartbreak. The more Nell described what Mallory had done to her, the more Sebastian asked her to talk about her own "pent-up anger" instead.

"I don't have any pent-up anger!" she finally screamed.

The room went silent. Nell drooped in her chair, her eyes steadily focused on the floor. She didn't move or say a word for the rest of the session. Neither did Mallory.

Although he had made a friend through this therapy group,

and although Sebastian had convinced him that he was not as much of a loser as his father had always told him he was, the thought of Nell castigating him in front of the whole group every week was too much. He decided this would be his last meeting.

Chapter 10: Going Viral

"We have 45,000 followers on Instagram. Our *Nell* trope is going viral. And we have a sponsorship deal on X for $100 a post next month. You're a hero! You're an absolute hero."

"I haven't done anything."

"Haven't you seen your latest TikTok post, the ones with the five calico cats singing *Mercy Mercy*? Ten thousand likes in two days! And I have a friend who's coming up with a jingle to go with that Mad Mallory character. A jingle is exactly what we need. But I'm going to start calling him Manic Mallory. We have to keep changing, coming up with new stuff to keep people's attention. And it's working. Things are going great."

"So, when will I get my $100?"

"Not yet. Not yet. But listen, I haven't even told you the biggest thing. Remember those people in Dallas I told you about? They're called American Values. They say they can get us hundreds of thousands of followers. Maybe millions. And they might get some political ads for us from candidates who agree with our philosophy. We have to go down to Dallas next week to seal the deal. They love your attitude. They want to meet you personally."

"I have a job. I have two jobs."

"Look, Kevin. Nobody ever made their fortune answering calls for UniCast Cable. Or working for a car dealership. This is your big chance to break out of these meaningless jobs. You've got to take this chance!"

"But, if I did go, what would I say?"

"Don't worry about that. I'll take care of that."

"I mean, what would I say to UniCast and Lou's Lexus?"

"Just call in sick."

Mallory had learned from the Ms. Marcie affair that UniCast had absolutely no sick leave. Any time missed for any reason was subtracted from your vacation. Consequently, he had always found himself well enough to show up for work and at least slump down in his chair even when he wasn't feeling well. He had no idea what Lou's Lexus's sick policy was. But Spike told him they wouldn't have to leave until next Friday, and he didn't start at Lou's until the following Monday.

"I'll still lose a day of vacation from UniCast."

"If we hit it big, your life will be a continuous vacation."

He said he would go. He dreaded telling Kathie. They had both been unusually quiet during their commute since the day she had hugged him. As badly as he wanted to find out all about her, he didn't know how to start. She seemed embarrassed that she had hugged him and gotten him all excited. He decided she had probably done it by mistake. Things between them were just too messy to clear up so quickly. And he knew she disapproved of his internet adventures. He decided to put off the Kathie issue until he got back from Dallas.

Chapter 11: Desperately Seeking Simone

Mallory had never been on a plane, or stayed in a hotel, or left the state of Maryland. He had been away on vacation only once. His parents had taken him at the age of six to Ocean City. He still remembered his excitement the first time he was knocked down by a wave and held underwater by the current. He still remembered bravely fighting his way up, gasping for air, looking around, wishing his parents were watching. He remembered they went out to the beach only twice that week. He guessed that was normal. He remembered they quarreled a lot, especially on the long ride home, but that wasn't anything unusual.

The tickets were paid for by the American Values group in Dallas. Spike made all the arrangements and led Mallory through all the rigmarole in both airports. Mallory had imagined that riding in an airplane would be luxurious, but he found himself yearning for the comfort of his cubicle at UniCast. He didn't realize you could order drinks until they were halfway there. They didn't have any cognac, but he made do with a couple orders of Dewars doubles. He had a cramp in his foot off and on, and his back was aching by the time they landed in Dallas. They took a rental car to get to the hotel, the same hotel where they would meet with the potential sponsors that afternoon. Their suite was spectacular, his room fancier and more comfortable than any he had ever been in.

The bed was especially soft. He lay down on it, ignoring Spike's advice to keep awake for the meeting that was supposed to begin in an hour. His room had a large TV, and Spike had assured him they would have a porn channel. But he could no longer afford Simone, and he couldn't afford to subscribe to any of the hotel's porn sites, so he left the TV off. Mostly, he yearned for contact with a real woman, mostly Kathie. He tried to imagine being in bed with her, and he kept coming back to that brief hug in his doorway. That had really happened. That was real, unlike Simone.

He saw a small refrigerator underneath the television and opened the door. He couldn't believe his eyes. There was a whole mess of tiny bourbon and scotch bottles in the minibar! He opened three and put more in his pockets. What a hotel! He knew he owed it to himself to drink as much of the free booze as he could as he waited to be called into the meeting.

Spike had advised him to freshen up, but Mallory was lost in his reverie, trying to imagine in his head the prurient pictures he couldn't afford to see on the screen. A woozy image of Simone wended its way into his half-dream. As he continued sipping his scotch, his mind was swirling with resentment that he was the only real man he knew who was being forced to be celibate.

Spike looked appalled at Mallory's condition when he came to the room to bring him to the meeting. "At least, change into some better clothes."

"I didn't bring any clothes."

"Look. Okay. Just don't say anything while we're in there. These people can give us everything we would ever want."

"The only thing I got so far is $150 from you – and being priced out of Simone."

Spike just smirked.

The meeting took place in a conference room on the first floor.

"Welcome, Mr. Mallory, to the American Values Group. We at the Group are great admirers of your forthright defense of our traditional American values."

"If you don't mind my butting in," Spike butted in, holding out his arm in front of his partner to keep Mallory from answering. "We espouse these values because we too believe America is being destroyed by the LGBT+ movement and by corporate cancel culture. Elite media types are ramming their WOKE theories down our throats, teaching our children that transgenderism is normal.

"But" – Spike held up a finger to forestall any response – "what we offer is unique. We have created an internet presence like none

Mallory Meets His Match

you have ever seen before. Mr. Mallory is preaching this gospel to hundreds of thousands of followers. He has singlehandedly created a trope, the *Nell*, that helps people categorize certain types of lesbian indecency, and that term is already becoming part of our language. And that is just the beginning. We have an animated cartoon series starring Manic Mallory that is sweeping the nation."

Mallory was having a hard time staying awake.

"We realize you have had some success." The man in the middle of the three-person committee, a middle-aged man with a dark crewcut and a brown suit, seemed to be the spokesperson. "But we believe we can still be of much needed service to you. Your message is so on point, and so ... um ... *trenchant*, but it needs to be amplified. To get to the point, we can hook you up with at least a hundred other websites that we control that could amplify your message. Your audience can grow from thousands to millions. You do understand that an influencer like that can make a fortune."

"Well, we don't actually have that many ads yet."

"I guarantee you the American Values Group has connections that can flood you with ads."

"Okay." Spike leveled his eyes at each committee member, one at a time. "What is it you want in return?"

"It's very simple," the spokesperson answered immediately. "Our country needs new leadership, a man who isn't afraid to tell it like it is. American Values feels we know who that is. We're supporting Jake De Santo for president of the United States. We want Mr. Mallory's wholehearted support. Tweets, blogposts, Instagram, Facebook, YouTube, whatever. I'm no internet expert myself, but we have people ...."

"You mean politics?" Mallory was suddenly awake. He didn't understand any of this internet or business talk, but he knew what he believed. "Politics is what is ruining this country. I'm against politics." He heard Spike breathe out heavily next to him. "And I haven't got any money yet, except for $150. And now you've made my girlfriend, Simone, cost $99 a month. I don't have $99 a month.

I don't believe any of this fucking money talk. I want Simone. Nothing else. Give me Simone and I'll believe you guys are for real."

*** ***

Mallory dozed off at the start of the 100-mile limousine trip to Waco. When he woke up, he had a nagging headache, but he was in a great mood. He felt that things were starting to fall his way, and he gave himself credit for finally taking some steps to get what he really wanted.

"We'll be there in half an hour," Spike interrupted his reverie.

Now he was about to make one of his life dreams come true. After Mallory's outburst at the American Values meeting, Spike had taken the spokesperson aside. There had been a vigorous, hushed conversation between the two of them, then between Spike and the whole committee. The next thing he knew, they were in a limousine headed to Waco, the home of the real Simone de Boudoir.

"You have to report the money they gave you on your taxes, as a consultant fee," the driver drily reminded him now.

"Shit," Spike responded. "I can't believe that whore costs so much."

Mallory's only condition for going along with the American Values plan was a real, live encounter with Simone de Boudoir. There had been quite a flurry of phone calls and emails and internet research as they searched out where she really lived. The good news was that she made her home not 100 miles away.

"The price was ultra-exorbitant." Spike griped. "And now I have to pay taxes on that."

Mallory's head was feeling much better. "What a crazy trip." Now that his head was clearing, he thought he would have settled for a free subscription to Simone's website. But he couldn't help replaying in his head her yelps and cries that had been the background audio for so many of his fantasies.

The address seemed to be an appliance repair shop between an auto parts store and a laundromat in a strip mall on the outskirts of town. The driver got out to ask further directions, but he came back and said this was it. They walked in the door and through a narrow gap between a work van and a line of reconditioned washing machines for sale until they reached what the owner called "the safe room." It was actually just a walled, concrete patio behind the repair shop. There, right in front of Mallory's eyes, was the real Simone, sitting on a real mattress, holding a terrycloth robe tightly around herself. She looked nervous. Mallory felt nervous himself when he found out the appliance repair man was also her husband.

There was something that looked like a homeowner's surveillance camera screwed to the wall, pointing at the mattress. "No! No filming. Absolutely not!" Spike insisted. "Mr. Mallory is a famous icon, and he's not here to make a porn advertisement for you. For God's sake, isn't the money enough?"

Simone's husband looked like he'd been sticking his face inside broken washing machines for too many years. He suddenly brushed past Mallory and Spike and got into a truck in the parking lot and sped off, spitting gravel at them from his wheels.

Mallory had no idea what to say or do. His gaze wandered over toward Simone. She was sitting cross-legged on the bed, putting makeup on with a hand-held mirror. She paused and smiled at him – sadly, he thought. She wore her dark hair short now. Her skin was fair and her face was a little bit wider than he'd imagined, but she was still more beautiful in person than she had ever looked in her blurry website videos.

"Come on. Let's get out of here." Spike's insistent voice broke into Mallory's reverie. "Being in a porn video would ruin your whole American Values image."

Mallory disagreed. "What's more American than porn?" Boldly, he pushed his way past Spike and the driver and sat down on a chair at the side of the bed. He recognized the fleur de lis pattern on Simone's bedsheet from his many visits to her website. He was surprised at how hard the bed itself looked.

"Oh, it's just a mattress on a piece of plywood," Simone explained. "I need a sturdy platform to … you know." She continued putting on her lipstick, very slowly. Mallory was surprised that she seemed a little shy. She was definitely not the bold, everything-in-your-face tease she seemed online. As she pursed her lips together to smooth her lipstick on, he could feel his heartbeat even down below. He asked if she put makeup on her body, too. She nodded yes. He asked her if he could watch, and she nodded again. She started to put rouge on her cheeks very slowly, glancing over at him nervously at first, then rolling her eyes as his breath came faster.

He could hear Spike fuming behind him, but he couldn't focus on what was being said. Spike seemed to be arguing with their driver. Mallory hoped the argument would at least go on long enough for him to see the rest of Simone's preparations. When she dropped the robe off her shoulders and started rouging her breasts, he lost all control.

"I'm doing this, Spike, no matter what!"

"Okay. Okay, how about this?" Spike jumped between Mallory and the driver, speaking fast and loud to both of them at the same time. "You can film this, but we have to hide his identity. Blur out his face in the video. Anybody here know how to do that?"

Nobody answered.

"Just hurry up, please," Mallory begged. Simone was breathing faster, as if the argument were making her nervous. She slipped her bra and her robe back on just as Mallory was starting to appreciate the wondrous motions of her chest.

"Doesn't your husband know how to blur out a face?" he asked her.

"He doesn't want anything to do with this." Her voice was tiny. Her dark eyes were larger and softer than they looked on her porn site. Her wide smile looked familiar to him, but it lacked that lascivious look he was used to from her website.

"Doesn't your husband know what you do on the site?"

"Sure. We do it together. But it's just video. I've never …." She suddenly sat up straighter and let her robe drop. She seemed to be holding her breath. He watched her force a smile at him as she tossed the robe aside. Then she arched her back and posed for him until he was panting at the sight, the proximity, of her body. But he still wasn't on the bed yet. "We have to do this," she whispered. "The shop is being foreclosed on."

She looked into the camera lens and slowly fingered her black, almost transparent lingerie, dropping her bra first, then slowly moaning as if that new freedom to caress herself gave her a surge of relief. Then she worked more slowly down below, so slowly that Mallory, watching, lost all track of his surroundings.

Her moans and cries were so convincing he was afraid she was going to finish without him. He decided he totally loved her. Then Spike came back carrying a baseball cap, sunglasses, and a Covid mask that the driver had found in the glove compartment. "Put this crap on or I'll smash that camera!"

Spike tossed the paraphernalia at him. At that point, Mallory would have done anything to make sure Spike didn't interfere. Simone was now lying on her back, whimpering, and crying out as she conducted her own anatomical explorations.

Then she stopped and slowly stretched her arms above her head and laid them back on the mattress. Mallory was suddenly worried that she had already worn herself out. She went quiet and stared at him as if she had no idea what to do next. "Mr. Ramsteel, aren't you ready?" He sat on the bed, leaned across and traced the tips of his fingers across her wondrously flat stomach, hip to hip. Her only reaction was to let out a deep sigh. He thought he might have already waited too long when he saw a trace of tears in her eyes.

"What's wrong?"

She looked away from him without responding.

"Am I too fat?" he tried.

He had actually lost some weight in the last few months. That

71

wasn't it.

"Is it this hat and the sunglasses and the mask?"

She turned back to him, shook her head. He thought back over their relationship. He usually put out of his mind anyone else's problems if those problems didn't immediately affect him. But he tried to focus now on what was making her so sad. The meaning of what she had said earlier finally came to him.

"You've never done this before, have you?"

"Right, Mr. Ramsteel. I told you that. But I agreed to do it now."

He felt like he was separating into two parts. His head and his heart did not want to make this woman do something she was deeply ashamed of, but from his belt on down he'd never been so excited. And she had already surrendered. The choice was up to him.

Chapter 12: Head Problem

Mallory's moment of satisfaction gradually faded over the next few hours, and as his plane descended toward BWI-Marshall airport, tingles of anxiety began to creep up his legs. Kathie had told him she didn't want to hear anything more about *God's Truth*, and so he hadn't told her anything about American Values, or the *Nells* either. He hadn't told her he was going to Dallas. And, in an attempt to simplify his communications with her, he hadn't told her he wouldn't be coming in to work at UniCast on Friday either.

He called her when he got back home on Saturday night, but she didn't pick up. Spike had cancelled their meeting at the Dough and Go that night. He called Kathie again, but she didn't answer. They didn't usually talk on weekends, so he had always assumed she was carrying on a hot affair with some other man. After hearing about Rhys in Building Management and an ex of hers at Lou's, he feared there would be a ghost of an ex every place he went.

She called him Sunday morning. "What the hell! Where were you Friday? When you didn't show up in the parking lot, I went to your door, but you didn't answer. Your neighbor across the way didn't know where you were. We talked about breaking down your door. I was an hour late for work."

He hadn't realized she would notice that he was gone. He was too surprised now to make up a story. "I was on a trip."

"You didn't realize I was coming to pick you up, like I have every day for the last two months?"

"Um."

"You basically forgot about me, didn't you?"

Kathie was right, but he didn't want to say that. Earlier in his career he had often used the sudden death of a grandmother as an excuse for being absent. His grandmother had died seven or eight times during his many jobs. But his mind was now squirming for an answer that wouldn't be a total lie.

"I did forget to tell you. Because it was an emergency."

"Oh." Her voice went soft. "Did somebody die?"

He just couldn't kill another grandmother. Then he realized there was something he could say that wasn't entirely false. In fact, there was a kernel of truth in it. "No. I met up with a woman I used to be involved with."

"Oh." Her single soft syllable seemed to straddle the line between jealousy and relief.

"We settled everything. It's totally over now."

"Oh. Oh. I guess that really is none of my business. Sorry to rag on you. But from now on, please let me know if you're not going to need me in the morning."

"What if I need you at night?"

"Oh, stop it." She hung up.

*** ***

Mallory stood next to a little wooden stand at the entrance to the service department at Lou's. They had promised him a desk, but they said they were moving things around and it wasn't ready yet. He asked for a chair, and they said they'd get it to him by the next day. One of the mechanics, or "service technicians," as they were called, approached. He was a young guy, not too tall, dirty blonde hair, an absent look in his eyes as if he didn't see Mallory at all. Without a word, he handed Mallory a torn-off piece of a brown plastic bag with the words "blue ES 330 hd gask needs time belt" written in it. As there were only three cars in the shop at the moment, and only one was blue, Mallory figured that the mechanic had worked on that one. He looked that car up on his computer terminal and found the record of the car coming in: "2006 ES 330 blue, hd gask."

Mallory wanted to succeed at this job, if only to keep Kathie's interest up. He had no idea what "hd gask" or "time belt" meant. He realized that he'd have to turn around, walk across the dirty service floor in the dim light of the service section, find the blonde-haired kid, and ask him what the message meant. He sighed at all the effort that would take, but then he bravely walked across the floor anyway and spotted the kid doing something underneath a car on a lift. But Mallory couldn't seem to get his attention, even after he coughed and made a few other noises with his mouth. He looked around behind him and saw a bright red cabinet with lots of thin steel drawers. One of the drawers was open. He picked out the biggest steel wrench in the drawer and threw it down hard on the concrete floor next to the mechanic.

"Ouch! Jesus, why'd you do that?" The kid came out from under the car, rubbing his head. Mallory didn't know if it was a question he should answer or not.

"Um, could you tell me what this thing you wrote here means, head band or something?"

The kid didn't have to look at the note. "Yeah. The new head gasket I already put on. But the guy needs a timing belt, too."

"Okay." Mallory felt empowered. "Thanks."

Mallory realized later he probably should have anticipated the customer's reaction when he gave him the news. "Sir," he began, trying to sound cheerful. "Your head gasket's been replaced. The cost is $1,890 for that. But when we looked at your car, we also found that you also need a timing belt. We need your permission to do that. That's gonna cost another $750."

"What? My car was running fine until the head gasket went up."

"Well, sir, we checked the timing belt and it's ... *broken*, too. You probably shouldn't drive the car in that condition."

"Absolutely not. I want my car back as it is, with just the new head gasket."

"Um, okay, I guess."

"When can I pick up the car?"

"I'll have to check on that."

75

The blonde mechanic was even deeper into the innards of a car, so Mallory wandered out into the showroom and found the office of Rick Gunther, who had hired him. He explained the situation. "When can I tell him he can pick up his car?"

The answer seemed to be more complicated than he had anticipated. Gunther got up from his desk and followed Mallory back to the service area, told him to wait there, then crossed the floor in search of the mechanic. He came back a minute later. "Call the customer, tell him he really needs the timing belt, and we can do it for $575."

Mallory assumed the customer would be happy, but the customer still said he didn't want the timing belt. By this time, Mallory had Rick Gunther's extension, and he just called him.

"Still couldn't make the sale, huh? You know, your one percent commission shrinks every time a customer turns us down. Tell you what. Call him back. Tell him we can do the damn timing belt for $350."

The customer finally accepted that deal. Mallory joyfully strode across the floor and playfully tapped the mechanic on the back. "The customer just accepted the deal. When can you get started putting in the new timing belt? I need to call him and tell him when it will be ready."

"I put it in yesterday."

*** ***

Mallory didn't want to fail at his new job because of Kathie. She got him the job and she drove him there every day, and he felt like it was almost her job, too. But it was beginning to look like he soon wouldn't need the money from Lou's. At least, that's what Spike said.

"We have a possible deal with American Values! Twenty bucks a tweet or post to start. Five tweets a day. Three posts a day each on

TikTok and Instagram. Two posts on Facebook. And they got us a dog food company, Bowser Gourmet, to run a commercial linked to your every post on *God's Truth*. American Values believes the same things we do – and they're willing to pay for it!" Spike took a breath, went on in a calmer voice. "But you're going to need to wear a suit."

"What?"

"Look, your followers love your tweets and posts. They especially love Manic Mallory. You're growing exponentially, but only online. Meanwhile, the mainstream media is falling all over itself to follow every LGBTQ+ and WOKE angle they can think of, but totally ignoring Manic Mallory. American Values can help us to break out of the pack, conquer the mainstream media as well, make a fuss they can't ignore."

"I don't think so."

"Kevin, you saw in Dallas how they throw money around. That hookup with Simone de Boudoir was probably one of the most expensive hookups of all time. I want to offer you to them, as a real person, a Kevin Mallory that the mainstream press will not be able to ignore. I think I can get real money from them for that."

"Um …."

"How about this? A trial run. One public speech. We'll tell American Values we'll do it, and the price will be paying off all your credit cards."

Chapter 13: Mommie Dearest

When Kathie told Mallory she wanted to meet his mother, Delores, he cringed at the thought. "Believe me. You don't want to do that."

"She lives right in town. Don't you ever talk to her?"

"I used to, every once in a while. She's mad at me now." But Mallory had learned in the last few weeks that Kathie would not accept such a flat statement as an adequate answer, so he went on. "Um, it's a lot of things. She had a work friend who she was pushing on me. It didn't work out between us. My mother blames me." Mallory stopped after reciting these bare, true facts. He was hoping that Kathie wouldn't push to know more. He hoped that their relationship had reached that sweet spot where she wanted to know a little about his past life with women – but without pressing him for all the sordid details.

"What was her name?"

"Rose."

"That's a pretty name."

When Kathie stopped there, he breathed a sigh of relief. He liked that she didn't feel the need to examine his every thought. Some of his thoughts were not so good, he knew. He knew because his mother had told him that all his life. The only reason his father gave him for leaving was his mother's "picking, picking, picking at my head all the time." As Mallory grew into adolescence and later into young adulthood, he felt he understood what his father meant. But at least his mother hadn't abandoned him. When his father died fifteen years after he had abandoned his family, nobody had bothered to notify him. Mallory had no brothers, sisters, aunts, uncles, or cousins. Kathie knew his mother was his only living relative.

"What about your father? Did he start a new family after he left?"

"If he started a new family after he left, no one ever mentioned it to me."

"Wow." Kathie's voice was apologetic. "I didn't mean to drag up all this dirt."

"Yes, you did." He turned to her. He couldn't help smiling "But I don't mind telling *you* all this bad stuff. It's, like, easy to do."

Their excuse for visiting Delores was that he needed her to repair one of his suits so he could make his one public appearance for American Values. One pair of suit pants had been torn when the SWAT team had thrown him down on the parking lot of the courthouse. The other had been torn in his late-night confrontation with the man who had come to repossess his Escalade. At the time, he hadn't bothered to respond to his mother's offer to repair them because he had decided he couldn't afford to wear them anyway because of the dry cleaning bills.

"Nice to meet you, Kathie." But Delores's voice was icy.

"Nice to meet you, too. I've heard a lot about you."

At this statement, Delores shot a look at Mallory. Then she just nodded towards the chair Kathie could sit down in.

"Not pretending to be a lawyer anymore, I hope," Delores began. "You could have gone to law school, you know, if you'd made any effort."

"Thanks for the advice." Mallory's sarcasm was obvious.

"It's thanks to me, you know, that you got as far as you did in school."

"It's thanks to you I hated every minute of it."

"Let's look at these suits," Kathie jumped in. "This one's pretty badly ripped at the knee. Do you think it's salvageable?"

He had told her in the elevator she didn't have to talk to the old bird at all. And Kathie usually wasn't one to feel she needed to fill in any gaps in the conversation. He was surprised that she did now.

Delores inspected the pants. "Omigod. These are both quite a mess. One of these tears will have to be rewoven. I can do it, of course."

"That's impressive. Where did you learn that, Delores?" Mallory had never seen Kathie suck up to anyone before.

"Used to work at a dry cleaners, honey. Years ago. When they had full service. You wouldn't remember that."

Kathie didn't seem to feel the need to go any further with the conversation.

"Why are you getting these pants fixed, after all this time?" his mother asked.

"I'm going to start wearing them to work again. I can afford to get them cleaned now. I have a second job."

"If you'd have stuck long enough in any of the jobs you had …."

"Kevin is doing very well in both of his jobs," Kathie interrupted.

Delores jerked her head and squinted at the brash younger woman. The lines gravitating down from the corners of her mouth deepened. "You don't understand the problems …. You don't know his long history, honey."

"I know he's doing very well in his present circumstances – *with the people he hangs with now.*" Kathie gave Delores a withering look, and she hesitated for only a second before she went on. "He seems to be overcoming the trauma of how he was raised."

"You don't know anything about how he was raised," Delores snapped back, then clamped her mouth shut. She and Kathie stared at each other. Then Delores turned her attention to the pants. The women didn't speak to each other for the rest of the visit.

"I know I encouraged you to go see her," Kathie said as she drove him home. "But she's a real bitch, isn't she?"

Mallory just laughed.

"No," she stopped him. "I mean it. Take it from somebody who's been called a bitch more than once. I mean, your life has been so different. My mother was everything to me. To me and Dana and Jim. When we lost her, I felt like I was going to die. But the thing is, we did have her, once, and that makes all the difference. You know what I mean?"

He wished he did. But he didn't.

Kathie dropped him off at his apartment where he lived alone, still as sexually frustrated as ever. He wasn't experiencing fantasies of Simone anymore, and he had no interest now in going to her website. When he had visited her in Texas, he had bonded with her in a different way than he had expected. Seeing her turn on and turn off her faux orgasms on cue had been fascinating, but not as exciting as when he had thought it was the real thing. He had still been plenty excited. But in the end, he hadn't had the heart to turn this faithful housewife of a washing machine repairman into a prostitute.

They had gone through a simulated sexual union, complete with yelps and cries from both participants, only because Mallory didn't want to lose face with Spike. He hoped Spike hadn't watched too closely. Simone had done her best to vocalize the requisite female moans and screams, but she couldn't help smiling, and even once laughing, on camera. It was going to be a very strange sex video.

But Mallory was still confused about Kathie. She had hugged him once, but that hadn't led anywhere. He wondered who she'd been out with on Saturday night. He did enjoy the fact that Kathie seemed to dislike his mother as much as he did. But otherwise, he just felt confused and lonely. And whenever he felt that way recently, he looked for answers on *God's Truth*.

God's Truth was certainly right about Nell. She had humiliated him long ago by feigning interest in him, getting him to cat sit for her while she was secretly pursuing a hopeless lesbian relationship with Kathie. And she would never forgive him for being friends with Kathie now. Her attempt to humiliate him in the Healing Hearts had failed. Ever since that therapy meeting, she seemed even more bitter, her pale face pulled tight with animosity whenever she came near him. Even though Mallory kept mum about the *Nell* trope, word of this new addition to the English language eventually spread throughout UniCast Cable anyway. Although the company officially assured her that this insult would have no effect on her evaluation, her all-volunteer Cheer Committee lost three of its seven members, and no one would speak to her about their cats anymore. Then Nell filed suit, blaming the company for the whole thing.

Kathie told him she had tried to mend fences with her, but Nell had been too upset to talk. She asked Mallory to try. He was too afraid.

Then, surprisingly, even Harrison asked him to try to calm her down.

"Why would I try to calm that bitch down?"

"For the company's sake." Harrison went on even as Mallory smirked. "Okay, for *my* sake. I won't survive in my position here if there's one more problem coming out of this unit."

"I don't know." He was enjoying seeing Harrison beg.

"Please think about it. She's blaming the company for the *Nell* thing, too. And you know, the word is UniCast is thinking about merging our entire operations here into the midwest office and laying off all our staff."

"I have plenty of other sources of income."

Harrison raised his salt-and-pepper eyebrows at that. "Oh. You do? I'd like to hear about that someday. But not now. Okay, but even if you have another source of income, what about your friend, Kathie? Would you like to see her lose her job?"

He hadn't thought about Kathie's job. He told Harrison he would talk to Nell.

*** ***

"Get out of my cubicle!"

Nell's reception was about what he'd expected. He carefully stepped back to the precise line delimiting the cubicle border. "I was asked to bring a message to you from the Healing Hearts Therapy Group."

"So, you're their spokesperson now? That's hard to believe."

"They know we work right next to each other."

"What's the message?"

"They want to apologize for making you feel uncomfortable," he lied. "Sebastian feels especially bad that you clammed up before you had the chance to adequately vent your feelings." Mallory was pretty sure that was the kind of thing Sebastian would say.

"I didn't go there to 'vent my feelings.' I went there to warn them about what a sleazebucket you are."

"They already knew all the bad stuff about me."

"Then I can't believe they even let you stay."

He met her eyes. "I think they started me on the path to healing my heart, Nell. Give them a chance to heal yours."

Chapter 14: School Daze

"No, I just can't do it." Mallory felt uncomfortable with the whole idea of anything to do with school. He had horrible memories of being so alone for so long among so many kids, of being ridiculed for being fat, of teachers looking down at him with thinly disguised pity.

"Mr. Mallory, you have to step out of your comfort zone." Spike looked like he wasn't sure Mallory understood that concept. He went on. "In other words, get out of your rut. This is how we go big time. Speaking before the school board in a public meeting is the ideal way to really go big. Here, read the speech I gave you."

Mallory read the single page printed in 24-point type.

"Oh my God! Is this really true?"

"Honest to God's truth."

"Somebody should stop this."

"Think about it. You might be the only one who can."

Two days later, Mallory found himself speaking in front of the Howard County Board of Education. "If you don't know me," he began, "you should. Your children do." The printed speech shook in his hands. He hadn't thought much about school since he'd escaped it. He had no sympathy for any of the people who had been his onetime classmates. But he was shocked by what the LGBT-plusses and WOKEs were doing to today's kids. And Spike had told him he was the only person with the power to stop it.

"I'm one of the biggest influencers in the country. Millions of people read my posts and tweets and listen to my podcasts every day. And now I'm bringing my insights directly to all the parents of kids in the Howard County public schools.

"I'm speaking out about the horrible indoctrination of our children that is going on right now in our schools. Our children are being taught, not that God created them male or female, but that there are seven sexes, L, G, B, T, Q, plus the regular ones. They are taught that no children can just assume they are normal."

"Mr. Mallory, where, exactly, is this happening?" The female board member who interrupted him was an old, bent-over woman with nothing but a short skullcap of leftover, desiccated, yellowing hair. Her face was pretty much hidden behind a pair of huge, rose-tinted glasses. In his previous life, Mallory would have totally ignored any comments from such an unattractive person, but he realized that he was part of a critical social movement now. He had to act professionally. But he couldn't think of any specific schools where this was happening. In fact, he didn't even know the name of a single school in the county. He decided to just keep reading his speech.

"Any children who insist they are just regular boys and girls are interrogated in front of the class. They are forced to write essays on how they will cleanse themselves of their so-called discrimination against the whole rainbow of deviance that is now being taught as normal."

The chair of the school board, a middle-aged man with a tired slump to his posture and a worn business suit, dropped his pencil and sighed loudly into the mike. "Mr. Mallory, this board has not heard of any such incidents. Do you have any specific examples where anything like this at all has happened in any of our schools?"

"I'm glad you asked that question." Mallory was glad Spike had prepared him well. He pulled out the page marked "Response" in bold red letters at the top of his stack. "I can't give you any specifics, and I'll tell you why. This is all being suppressed by the school bureaucracy. These administrators have themselves been indoctrinated ever since college. They come from elitist schools where the idea of a man and a woman being created differently is considered chauvinistic, where a male student who calls a woman pretty is punished by the administration. These academics live in their own world and never have to face the public like you school board members do. They never face the public because they know their doctrines contradict the values that all real Americans hold dear."

Mallory pounded on the podium, as rehearsed, and stomped out of the room. Spike gave him a thumbs-up from the back of the room and pointed toward a different door. They were followed out by a small crowd of people, including a news cameraman. Spike turned Mallory around to face the group. Two of the people, obviously reporters, shouted questions at him. Mallory was shaking, and sweating, but he remembered Spike's advice not to respond to any questions and not to say anything at all until the camera lights came on. When the lights came on, he read the words Spike had prepared for him.

"Soon there won't even be any such thing as a *family*. It's already beginning, right in our schools. Our children are being indoctrinated. They are told that their sexual organs are just a suggestion, and they should experiment with sex roles back and forth, back and forth, until perversion seems so normal to them their little minds no longer have any concept of morality.

"All of our children are forced to celebrate this deviance in the name of anti-discrimination. The LGBTQs, together with the WOKES, are tearing down our whole idea of family to create a dystopian world where nothing matters but their elitist doctrine."

Mallory slumped over in exhaustion. But he was proud of himself for getting to the end of the speech. He had previously had no idea how bad things were in the schools. He was glad Spike not only told him about this but also gave him a chance to speak out in public about it. And he did like the idea of his speech being broadcast. He had always had a lot of opinions that nobody paid any attention to, but now at least some of these opinions were going to be on television.

"American Values is *extremely* happy with your speech," Spike told him two days later at their Saturday meeting. "I told them about your credit card debts. They're thinking about paying them off. I'm asking them to pay you cash for your next speech."

"Next one?" Mallory hadn't been planning on a next one. He

already felt rich, what with his credit cards possibly being paid off, and the extra salary soon coming in from Lou's Lexus.

"We'd ... you'd be a fool to stop now. Your clip on the local news was picked up by CNN, and the commentators on it went crazy. Then NBC and ABC both started a segment on the trending criticism of our schools' indoctrination of children. They included the entire clip of your speech at the school board meeting. We had a 50% jump in our Instagram and X followers overnight. Synergy! We are really making it big. American Values is hinting they'll pay for you to appear at political rallies, too."

"You know, Spike, I didn't realize all this horrible stuff was happening to our children. I should have paid more attention to *God's Truth* the last few weeks. I think I would do this for free, just to get the word out."

"Oh, no. We're not doing anything for free."

*** ***

"How do you like it at Lou's?" Kathie was driving him to work again. She seemed to have forgiven him for not telling her he was going to be out of town when he went to Dallas.

"I'm just getting started. The place is a little confusing sometimes."

"Maybe just hang in there, Kevin. Every job is confusing the first couple of weeks." She turned and looked at him at the next stoplight. "Take your time to get to know what's going on. Sometimes you seem to jump to conclusions without thinking things out."

The light turned green, and she moved her eyes back to the road. He was glad she didn't harp on this supposed fault of his. He had been told something like this before. Once, after he had carried a box of bullets around for months because he couldn't get the container open, Officer Selby had told him that the first step in solving any problem was to make a plan. The second step was to get whatever tools you needed. It wasn't exactly the same thing Kathie had said, but he was getting the idea that maybe, in general, it would be a good idea to think ahead before he acted.

But he was about to do something without thinking ahead. He was enraged about the way schools were treating kids. And he was energized by the possibility of making big money from exposing it. He was too excited to think ahead about how this would affect his relationship with Kathie. As she was a woman, he just assumed she'd be bowled over by the prospect of a man making millions. "Kathie, this internet thing of mine is really going big."

"You mean the *Nell* thing? You should be ashamed of yourself for that."

He jerked his head over to catch her eye, but she was looking at the road. He didn't understand why, if she thought what he did was so awful, she was still helping him, every day.

"I *am* ashamed of the *Nell* thing," he admitted. "I had no idea it would go that far. Spike is in control of the whole internet thing. He says we got a lot of hits on the *Nell* thing, but I told him to stop, and now he says we've moved on."

"Moved on to what? What are you doing?"

"Trying to save America."

"You?" She shook her head until her curls rustled. Her wide smile was just short of a laugh.

"Not all by myself. There's Spike, of course. And there are thousands of God's Martyrs. I'm a God's Martyr myself, you know. And there are millions of people online who are being shut out by the WOKE people and the LGBTQ-plusses. The WOKE and LGBTQ-plusses are being given everything, and people like you and me are being shut out."

They drove another mile on the crowded suburban highway before she spoke.

"Are these the same groups who are saying teachers are telling kids they have to choose what sex they are?"

"You heard my speech? Great! So you know what I'm talking about."

"Yeah. And I think it's all batshit crazy."

He wasn't surprised at her reaction. She was uninformed. It wasn't her fault. He wished he could get her to spend just one night on *God's Truth*. But, no matter how ignorant she was, he couldn't help how he felt about her.

"I know you think I'm crazy. But I still love you," he blurted out.

She pulled to a quick stop on the shoulder of the highway just in front of Lou's. She seemed oblivious to the cars whizzing by. "Kevin, I think you're a good man, deep down. But …."

"When you hugged me, I thought all my dreams were coming true."

She sighed. "I guess I shouldn't have done that. That was kind of a spontaneous thing. You had been helping me all day …."

This was just what he had feared. Her hug had been just a kind of tip. A girlie tip, given out without a thought of how much it might affect him. He hung his head, studied his hands. Officer Selby's words came to mind again: think about what you want first, then figure out the steps it will take to get there. Instead, he had just jumped ahead and asked for what he wanted more than anything else in the world, and the whole thing had blown up in his face.

"Maybe I'll keep the job at Lou's, even when I get rich. I'll try to do it right, just to show you I can."

"I would really like that."

Chapter 15: Flushed and Confused

Harrison seemed out of focus. He had asked Mallory to see him in his office without asking Peggy or anyone else to come in with him. "Sit down."

Mallory obeyed. Mallory was not exactly a figure of fashion himself, but even he noticed Harrison's disheveled look.

"I've got bad news for you, Mr. Mallory."

"Oh yeah?" Mallory was already devising counterattacks in his mind.

"I just got a call from Randy McNalley, the head of corporate human resources. I've been told to let you go."

"*You* did this!"

"No. I swear. I had nothing to do with it. Remember? I tried to warn you. Corporate is tired of your shenanigans. And I think Rhys is telling tales up the corporate ladder. But the last straw was your phony story on X about UniCast denying you a promotion because you aren't black or gay or trans."

"Nell must have something to do with this."

"No. Believe me. I asked."

Mallory had never really believed that anybody could be fired from UniCast Cable. Although he had long taken credit for saving the jobs of the less-than-mediocre employees he had defended, he had always assumed that UniCast was too big and bureaucratic to fire anybody anyway. But he could tell that Harrison himself was shaken by this new development, and he sensed that there was nothing either of them could do to change it. He stood up and turned to go.

"They told me I could give you three weeks' notice," Harrison said to his back. "I had to fight them even for that." Mallory slowly trudged as far as the doorway, but Harrison called him back. "You know, Mr. Mallory, I'm starting to understand the attitude you've displayed toward UniCast all this time."

"Those tycoons." Mallory spat out the words. "They don't care about regular people. They don't care about anything but piling up so much money even their great-great-great grandchildren will never have to work."

"So true." Harrison met his eyes. "You know, Mallory, I do hate to be the hatchet man for this fucking company. And it's only a matter of time before they fire me, too." Harrison gave Mallory a droopy smile. "Tell you what. I'll tell Ms. Marcie to sit on your paperwork, indefinitely. I don't care what Corporate says. You can stay here at UniCast until they kick my ass out the door."

*** ***

WOKE CORPORATION CANS CHILDREN'S CHAMPION !!! Popular blogger Kevin Mallory was fired today from his job as an employee representative at the UniCast Cable Company for expressing his views on social media and speaking out at a meeting at the Howard County School Board.

"I care about our children," Mallory responded on X and Instagram and Facebook and YouTube. *"They should not be forced to shop around for what sex they want to be under the so-called guidance of our WOKE teachers in Howard County. Somebody else has already made that decision. God!*

"SHAME on UniCast Cable for trying to muzzle me. They will never silence the voice of a true and free American crying out against this outrage!"

"Actually," Mallory complained to Spike, "they fired me for that other post, the one where I said I applied for a job and didn't get it."

"*Details*. Didn't I tell you not to get lost in the details? UniCast is terrified of not being WOKE and LGBTQ-plus enough. Look at the shows they're promoting on cable. Didn't you notice that half of them are showing guys kissing guys or teenage girls going through sex change operations?"

"Oh, I guess so." Mallory didn't really know. He couldn't afford UniCast Cable service.

Mallory was too depressed to care much about what Spike was doing. He spent more time thinking about his job at UniCast. Although he didn't like much of anything about UniCast, that job was his only connection to Kathie. He didn't tell her right away that he'd been fired. The next afternoon, when she mentioned that he looked depressed, he brushed her off. She said he was probably nervous about his new job at Lou's. She told him he'd get used to it. He didn't tell her any differently. He sat in the dark that night in the new chair she had given him. He was trying to imagine living his life without these conversations with Kathie.

He started thinking hard about what kind of person she was. She had dumped that creep Rhys and fought through his harassment. She had thought she loved Nell for exactly one night, then ended it painfully. She was good at her job, though she could fake it a little bit around the edges for a good cause. But he had never really asked her about her plans. He was ashamed that he hadn't found out anything about her parents, or about her brother or sister. But the one thing he had found out about her was, if she tried one thing and it didn't work out, she turned around and tried something else.

He told her truthfully it was Spike's fault he was fired, that Spike had posted an entirely fictitious story of him losing a promotion at UniCast because he was a white man. She said he should keep away from Spike, but then she cast her eyes down, as if she knew he wasn't going to take that advice, knew that Spike had just as much influence over him as she did. Mallory was shaken. "I think you're smarter than Spike," he offered. She smiled to herself but didn't answer.

He had guessed exactly what she would advise him to do, which was to focus on his new job at Lou's, keep his foot in the door, and keep his eyes open for any full-time openings there. That was exactly what he thought, too. At Lou's, he now had to learn how to deal with the beginnings of the transactions, when he had to tell the customers what was wrong with their cars and get them to agree to get the work done. It was more complicated than just taking the customers' original statements. Rick Gunther came out this day to show him the ropes in person. He was griping a little about having to stay late to do it. They still hadn't gotten an actual desk or chair, so Rick and Mallory stood uncomfortably together beside the little stand that was barely big enough to hold the company laptop. Rick showed him what had been written on the screen so far.

"Okay." Mallory thought he'd try to decipher the notes himself. *Thomasson. 2021 RC 350, black. 12,456 miles.*

"Little old lady car," Rick interrupted.

"Oh, do you know this Thomasson lady?"

"No. Mileage. Nobody who has a job drives only 6,000 miles in a year. A car with mileage that low, we call it a little old lady car."

"So, something's wrong with the car already?"

"Look on the screen."

Mallory read. "Customer ask check brakes."

Rick prompted him. "Now read what the service technician found."

"*Pads need repl.* I guess that means she needs new brake pads."

"What did he say about the rotors?"

"Um." Mallory scanned the mechanic's notes. "Nothing."

"Put this in, then: rotors (front) 1.063, (rear) .650. Need replaced."

Mallory was amazed that Rick could figure this out without even looking at the car. "So, how much should I tell her this is going to cost?"

"Pads are $100 a set. So, $200 there. Rotors are $200 each. So, $800 for four. That's $1,000 in parts. Labor is $750. So, $1,750 total for brakes."

Mallory hoped he would never have a brake problem if he ever got a car. But Rick wasn't finished.

"Okay. Now add oil change and filter."

"But it doesn't say anything here about an oil change."

"Little old lady car. Short little trips to the grocery store and the hairdresser. Degrades the oil fast. She needs it. Look up the price."

"$79."

"Okay. And now she needs to flush and fill her brake fluid."

"Oh, does that flush automatically go along with new brakes?"

"Yeah. Well, no. It automatically goes along with everything – but only as long as it's a woman's car."

"$250 for that. Right?" Rick nodded, but motioned Mallory closer.

"Let me explain something to you about my policies here. Some people don't think all the customers need all the stuff we sell them. Lexus might not. Lou might not. But that's how we do it in *my* shop. But if you mention any of this to Lou, or to any Lexus representative, I'll track you down and beat the living shit out of you."

Mallory didn't really understand what Rick was talking about, except for the part about getting the living shit beat out of him. But Rick kept staring at him, so he said "Okay, boss," and backed away from him as fast as he could.

*** ***

The new knowledge he had obtained from Rick, however, didn't help him much with Ms. Thomasson. This nice lady had readily agreed to all the improvements he recommended for her car. She was a quiet and polite woman, maybe in her fifties, slim, short, with neat, straight black hair streaked with grey. It took him a few days to realize that he liked her because she reminded him of Ms. Marcie. He carefully wrote up the work order exactly as Rick had told him to. He wanted to help her get her car in tip top shape, and as soon as possible.

Because she seemed to be such a nice lady, Mallory asked Victor, the mechanic assigned the job, to put her car in the front of the line.

Mallory Meets His Match

Victor didn't respond at all right then. But when Mallory asked him about it the next day, he told Mallory the parts department didn't have the right brake pads. Mallory had to call her and tell her she had to wait.

Two weeks went by. The first thing he did every day was to ask Victor about the parts. Every day Victor shrugged. "Can't do it without the pads." Ms. Thomasson told him her husband had taken his car on a business trip, and she needed her car to visit her daughter in Virginia, who was sick. Mallory asked Rick to give her a loaner car for a few days, but Rick said none were available.

Rick sounded exasperated. "What the hell's wrong with the parts department anyway? Can't they get a simple set of brake pads?" Mallory didn't know if that was a question he was supposed to answer. He left Rick's office and edged his way around the corner to the parts department. There was only one guy behind the counter at the parts department, and he was on the phone talking about car parts. Mallory didn't recognize the names of any of the parts he was talking about. He was glad he had brought his clipboard with the names of the parts Ms. Thomasson's car needed.

Finally, the guy hung up, but then he got busy typing something up on his computer, without looking up. Then another guy came in behind the counter and slid past the first guy. The new guy's name tag said "Steve." The first guy caught Mallory's eye and jerked his head. "Talk to Sludge." Mallory was confused. He was beginning to understood why the mechanics had so much trouble communicating with the parts department. He looked up, and Steve, or Sludge, finally made eye contact.

"Pads for that car?" Steve/Sludge acted surprised. "I'm sure we have pads for that car." He looked it up on another computer terminal. "We have eight sets of pads in stock right now that will fit that car." He made eye contact again. "Victor knows we have plenty of those pads. My guess is he doesn't like you."

*** ***

"It's much more complicated than I thought it would be," Mallory lectured to Kathie as she drove him home that night. "There's all kinds of stuff people's cars need that they don't know about."

"You're actually learning some new things. To me, it sounds a lot better than answering the customer assistance phone at UniCast."

"Yeah. I guess so." But his tone was grumpy. He was sometimes annoyed by her optimism for him. She never let him get away with blaming other people for his failures. That still irked him. But he took a minute now to think about what she was saying. "Maybe you're right. Maybe I'll have a car one day and need to know about the parts and all so I can …."

"You *will* have a car one day," she interrupted him. But then she gave him a wide smile. "And when you do, you're going to owe me a shitload of rides."

Was she planning on keeping him forever? Even after her charity work for him was done? He loved the way she talked sometimes so casually about their future, as if were a given that there would be a future. He suddenly felt the need to brag about his job at Lou's.

"I earned an eleven-dollar commission on just one car today. And guess what else I found out? There's this other company Flush-Rite, that will give me $25 cash for every brake flush I sell from now on."

"Oh, so you might make some money at that place after all. That's great. But it still sucks that you're getting fired from UniCast for that phony crap that *somebody else* posted."

Mallory recognized her dig at Spike, but he didn't dare respond.

Chapter 16: Manic's Panic

"You won't believe this!" Spike was practically yelling over the phone. "I couldn't wait until Saturday to tell you. Jake De Santo made a major speech in Atlanta today. He said you're a hero for pointing out that the public schools are indoctrinating our children."

"Who's Jake De Santo?"

"Don't you know anything? He's the famous senator from Florida. But, more importantly, he's also one of the front runners in the race for his party's presidential nomination."

"Oh, you know, I got my credit card bills again. You said they would be paid off."

"Yeah, yeah, I will get on them. American Values promised, and they won't dare cross us now. But listen, you don't understand how big this is. American Values has De Santo's ear, and they want you to appear with him at a rally, a really big rally, if he agrees."

"You said me speaking at the school board would be the last one."

"But you can't pass this up. You can become a national figure. You can earn hundreds of thousands of dollars as an influencer."

Mallory was starting to believe this might be possible. He was grateful to Spike. But he knew he hadn't received any money except for the $150 Spike had taken out of the cash register at the Dough and Go. And now he realized that, if he really was a national figure, he was powerful enough to make some demands on Spike. "Call me when my credit cards are paid off," he said, then hung up.

But it seemed that Spike was not making these things up. The following day, he received notice that one of his credit card debts had been paid off. And the following day, a beautiful, young, smartly dressed woman who introduced herself just as "Anne" appeared at his cubicle at UniCast and interviewed him about his hotel preferences in Atlanta. When he said he wasn't sure he was going, she leaned in so close their faces almost touched. He tried to inhale the scent of her perfume. He smelled only soap, but it was a nice, clean smell. She told him the campaign would fly him to Atlanta first class and pay for his meals and whatever other perks he desired. She whispered the word "perks" so breathlessly it seemed almost as if Simone de Boudoir were calling out to him. The thought of the real Simone made him smile. He was proud that he hadn't done her, and that American Values' money had gone to save the washing machine repair shop.

He told Anne he couldn't go because he had just started a job at Lou's Lexus. She immediately jumped up, took out her phone and said she'd be back in a minute. But Nell then suddenly appeared in his cubicle entrance. "Who the hell was that? Your taste in floozies is getting better."

He was surprised she was acting only halfway insulting. "Sorry, Nell. I can't help it if I'm attractive to *real* women."

"Does Kathie know you're floozing around on her?"

Mallory understood now. Nell was hoping he had a new girlfriend so she might get another chance with Kathie.

"For your information, Nell, that woman, Anne, is the person who decides where all the American Values money goes. And a big chunk of it is going to me because I am an influencer now. And Kathie is very supportive of my becoming an influencer."

Nell's face dropped, and she seemed to shrink down right in front of his eyes. "I see what you're doing online. That disgusting Manic Mallory cartoon character is making me sick." She was practically mumbling now. "You hate me, so you're taking it out on all lesbians and gays. I don't know about that school stuff, but that gay bashing is really sick. And what about blacks? As far as I know, your only man friend is black."

"Thomas has got nothing to do with it. Everything he got, he got on his own."

"Mallory, you're becoming part of the huge internet sicko-sphere now. I never thought that would happen. I never thought your shit-smell would stink up any more than your own cubicle."

"Oh!" Stylishly dressed Anne had just rounded the corner. She stopped short on hearing Nell's language. "Should I come back later?"

"No, come in," Mallory smiled. "This is Nell. She's the lesbian who killed my cat."

"Oh. *Nell*. Is that where that expression comes from?"

Nell stormed off. Mallory snickered to see her blow past her own cubicle in her rush to get away. He could now focus on the beautiful Anne, who was acting like he was an important person.

"Mr. Mallory, I just talked to Lou, the owner of Lou's Lexus. He's a supporter of American Values, and of all our causes. He agreed that you can take two days off to help us out in Atlanta. With full pay. Now, can we talk about your preferences in hotels and meals?"

*** ***

Spike told him he had a knock-down, drag-out fight with his father, who absolutely refused to give his son the two days off to make the trip. He also threatened to kick him out of house if he didn't stop driving Mallory's internet campaign.

"Oh, man, where will you go then?" Mallory knew he didn't have room for another person in his efficiency apartment, unless of course it was for a woman.

"That'll never happen. He'd never kick me out. But I have to keep on his good side. I have to. He's like, the patriarch of the whole family. You'll have to go by yourself."

Mallory was overjoyed to find out that Anne would be traveling with him. She bought first class tickets and arranged for them to travel together by Uber to the airport. She guided him through all the confusing online kiosks at the airport. She arranged his documents so they could get through security. They sat together in seats that were not as torturous as the economy seats he had been crammed into on the trip to Dallas. He liked Anne. She was as quick and precise as any businesswoman, but she had long, painted, pale blue fingernails and lush red hair, and she exuded a tense kind of sexual energy even through her black and white business suit.

He did tell Kathie this time that he would be gone for two days.

"Another breakup with another ex?" she asked, her eyebrows raised.

He didn't know what she meant. He wanted to brag to her that he was a success, that American Values was paying off all his bills, but he wasn't sure how she would take this. He was hurt that she didn't believe he could make it big in the internet world. He was hurt that she hadn't really responded when he said he loved her. His only relationship guide, Manly Man, had always said that those words worked like magic on women. But he hadn't been trying to seduce her when he said it. He had been just trying to tell her how important she was to him. But it seemed like he didn't mean that much to her.

"No," he finally responded. "This is a pure business trip. I know you don't want to hear about this internet thing. But it's really going good."

"Right. I don't want to hear about it. Be sure to keep your job at Lou's."

Anne now whisked him through the airport and to the hotel in Atlanta with even more aplomb than Spike had shown in Denver. "We have a meeting in an hour in the hotel restaurant with Raymond Schnapps, one of De Santo's top aides. Your speech is set for tomorrow. The rally begins at 5:30, and you'll be the first or second speaker. You have fifteen minutes. You and three other guys are sort of a warm-up for De Santo. He'll take the stage at about 6:15. You might have a chance to meet him if he arrives early."

"What'll I say to De Santo?"

"Well, I think you are here because you espouse the same values as Jake. Tell him how much you appreciate his exposing the elitist conspirators who are trying to demoralize regular people. Say hello to his wife, but don't touch her unless she extends her hand. And remember that he's reached out to you because he appreciates all you've done to help the cause. Oh, and be sure to mention that American Values sent you here."

They each had a drink in the hotel restaurant that evening while waiting for Raymond Schnapps to join them. They had started a second drink by the time he arrived. Mallory was impressed by his large frame, his hawk-like face framed by thick tortoise shell glasses, his impatient air. "Tell me, Mr. Mallory, what caused you to become an admirer of Senator De Santo?"

Anne had prepared him for his question. "Jake represents the values that made this country great. The American Values Group has urged me to come here to signify their support for his campaign for president."

"Good. Good. And can you tell me more about how you personally came to embrace these values?"

Mallory couldn't remember. It had something to do with Spike. "I have this social media guy back in Maryland. He helps me to say on the internet whatever I want. See, there was this lesbian at work, Nell, and she claimed I stole her cat, but I really didn't because the cat was mine, morally speaking, and I think it might have been a reincarnation of a ferret I used to have that had the same name, but spelled with *K*s instead of *C*s, and the SWAT team took my rifle at the courthouse even though it didn't have any bullets in it because I couldn't get the box of bullets open, and when the police came to my door my good friend Thomas threw the cat out the window, I mean, the window was low so KoKo didn't get hurt, but he was lost for a while, and …."

"I think I've heard enough," Schnapps interrupted. He turned to Anne. "American Values has already paid for him to be here?"

"Yes, exactly. They very much want De Santo to incorporate Mr. Mallory's views into his campaign. You must have noticed his massive internet presence and his exponentially growing list of followers."

"I see how Mr. Mallory's internet following might be of some value to the candidate, but …."

"Let me be utterly candid about this," Anne interrupted. "American Values believes that De Santo's heart is in the right place. But they also know he doesn't have the charisma to fire up the base. He needs the support of firebrands like Mr. Mallory if he's ever going to capture the attention of the base. And, frankly, Mr. De Santo has a lot of competitors who would jump at the chance to claim that Mr. Mallory supports them wholeheartedly."

Mallory hadn't heard of any other politicians who wanted his support. Anne hadn't mentioned anything like that to him. Twelve months ago, he would have believed anything this clever, competent, put-together woman said; but he had learned from his own experience that he was only one of many people who made their living shading the truth.

"American Values does have other options," she emphasized.

"Okay," Schnapps sighed. "American Values wants this guy to fire up the base. Mr. De Santo understands that. But we're adjusting the schedule as we go along. I'm going to put you on second, at 5:45, and just for five minutes. I hope you'll go over his speech with him tonight. I've got to get going now."

After he rushed out, Anne leaned across the table toward Mallory. "Do you have a prepared speech? I need to take a look at it?"

"It's in my room." Mallory said a prayer of thanks to Spike for shoving the speech in his hand as he left the Dough and Go two nights before. He was also thankful they'd have to get it from his room.

Anne didn't hesitate. "Okay. Let's go see it. And, oh, if your room is too messy or something, we can use my room."

His heart skipped a beat. "It's pretty messy."

Anne's room was not messy. If anything, her suite looked almost sterile. The bedroom door was closed, and all that was on the coffee table in the open room was a laptop and a huge pocketbook that looked like it could carry the Atlanta phone book, if there still was an Atlanta phone book. He thought she might take him more seriously if he started right in with the speech talk, but he couldn't help asking her first what was in the minibar.

"Oh, the usual stuff, like in any minibar, I guess," she responded. "Why don't you help yourself with whatever you want while I look over this speech?"

Mallory found a tiny bottle of cognac. He looked and found another one for her, but she held up one hand to ward it off. He noticed the swirl of those subtle blue nails, but the only thing those pretty talons were doing right then was holding him off. She was gripping Spike's speech tightly in the other hand while she scanned it. "I think this needs a lot of work. We have to shorten it to five minutes, for one thing."

"Okay." He realized she wasn't into him as much as into his speech. He sighed and melted down onto the sofa across the coffee table from her.

"This might be a little too gross for a televised speech," she started. "I think I can fix this. It shouldn't take more than an hour. Do you want to work along with me, or …? You look tired. You can just let me fix it myself, if you prefer."

Mallory woke up as she was arranging for the hotel to print out the revised speech. He then forced himself to keep himself awake until she returned fifteen minutes later with the manuscript. She handed it to him and asked him what he thought.

Mallory had recently come to the crushing realization that not every sexually mature female who voluntarily entered a room alone with him was craving his manly touch. Anne was not interested in his touch at all. He tried to focus on reading the heavily modified speech even as she held the paper in front of him with those lascivious pale blue nails. But the speech did get his attention.

The education establishment has been taken over by radical elements of the elites who wish to force their views on the children of regular Americans. Their aim is to create a society of undifferentiated clones.

Children should be able to call themselves boys and girls without any apologies ….

The speech was substantially toned down from the way Spike had written it. Something about it made Mallory nervous, but he knew she was a lot smarter than he was. He excused himself to go to his own room and study it. He waited a few extra beats before he stood up to go, giving her one last chance to take a personal interest in him. He had lost twenty pounds since his car had been repossessed, but he knew he still wasn't much more attractive than average. Anne, on the other hand, was off the charts. And she had bent that political manipulator, Schnapps, to her will. And she cared about the children as much as he did. They had a lot in common. But apparently, he didn't have everything that she needed.

They met for lunch Tuesday morning. Mallory ordered a cocktail. He didn't usually drink at lunch, but American Values was paying for everything. Then he thought he should make sure of that. "Of course," Anne assured him. "It's all on my company credit card." When he ordered another drink, she commented, "You're nervous, aren't you. That's only natural." She leaned closer. "But let me tell you about this type of crowd. They're not going to be critiquing every word you say. You don't have to convince them of anything. Half of them are already following you. They'll be thrilled just to see you in person."

"How many people are going to be there?"

"They sold 17,000 tickets in advance."

"Oh, my God." He looked over at his drink glass, which was empty again, but Anne shook her head: no.

"Really. Don't worry. Schnapps is going to introduce you as a hero to the movement. People will be screaming before you even say anything. They'll probably keep screaming no matter what you say."

But Mallory had another concern that he couldn't tell Anne

about. He didn't like her speech. He didn't want to use fancy words like *education establishment* or *undifferentiated clones*. That wasn't Spike's style at all. His followers on the internet wanted the plain *God's Truth*, he was sure. Together, they walked the short distance to the Georgia World Congress Center. Mallory told himself not to be afraid, but he knew he would be speaking in the week's biggest event in this massive complex. Anne was guiding him by the elbow through the early crowd. She took him to a large room converted to an office where Schnapps nodded to them above the small group of workers. He was standing next to a long table where other workers were signing people in and shouting orders. "All set," he said. "Mr. Mallory, you go on second, as planned. You speak for five minutes. Have you got your speech?" He turned to Anne before Mallory could answer. "Is this speech going to rev up American Values?"

"It's going to energize the base like De Santo himself could never do."

"No talk about ferrets, or Koko, or anything?"

"All set."

Anne steered him to the edge of the stage where he would speak. They waited almost a half hour for the first speaker, a home cooking show host, to show up. The man spoke for about twenty minutes. Mallory couldn't hear too much of what he was saying. He didn't think the crowd could hear much, either, but that didn't seem to make any difference. Every angry word, every mocking insult, every promise to "fry his ass" or "fricassee his behind" was met with roars of approval. Mallory didn't know who the man was talking about, but he was pretty sure it wasn't him, so he didn't pay much attention.

Schnapps took the mike and made a surprisingly peppy introduction for Mallory. "I guess a lot of you people know about *The Real Honest to God's Truth*." A small cheer rose from the crowd. "Well, we have here for you today a genuine Martyr of God and star of *God's Truth*, a man who has been speaking out against the WOKE crowd and the LGBTQ-plus crowd on every kind of social media, a man who personally exposed the horrific indoctrination of the children in his home county's public schools. Please give a warm welcome to internet influencer, LGBTQ-exposer and anti-WOKE hero, Kevin Mallory!"

Mallory had never imagined thousands of people cheering for him. He walked onto center stage and gave a wobbly wave to the crowd, but he wasn't prepared for the sudden roar that filled the venue. He looked back at Anne. She pointed to the screen behind him, where a huge cartoon image of Manic Mallory was projected. It was five times his actual size and sported the braided, beaded goatee he used to wear. It was animated by jerky, stylized facial expressions – eyebrows raised, tongue sticking out, one eye winking, etc. He recognized Spike's work. The entire crowd now seemed to love him. He decided to prance around the stage, from the far left to the far right and back again. The roar grew louder. He clapped slowly for himself and found the crowd clapping in unison with him. He had never believed Spike's claims that he was a hero until now.

He was having so much fun he forgot to be anxious about speaking. He decided that Anne's speech was too stuffy for the occasion. When the raucous introduction finally slowed down, he raised his hand. He felt an incredible surge of power as the crowd grew silent at his command.

"Did you know there are no girls or boys in our public schools anymore? There are no *hes,* no *shes*, just *theys*. I thought God created the sexes, but our schools are teaching our children that their sex is a choice they have to make. Our kids are being taught that their sexual organs are as changeable as Play Doh. And they are forced to play." Mallory felt a surge of energy as he remembered more and more of the things Spike had primed him to say.

"But that's not the half of it. You haven't heard the master plan being cooked up by the educational elite, the rainbow crowd and the WOKES, all working together to undermine the American values we all hold dear." Mallory could hear the crowd was with him, so he went on. "Your public schools will soon be harvesting sperm and eggs from your children and growing their babies in test tubes so that all newborn children will be anonymous, socially equal, and not stigmatized by association with any specific parents."

A loud chorus of boos urged him on. "In this colorblind, merit blind, heritage blind, parentless society, the geniuses and the half-wits will all get the same grades. The convicted murderer and the brave street cop will get the same honors. The little girl forced to become a boy will play football against the first-string linemen." The boos were loud enough now that Mallory decided he had accomplished his purpose. But there was one more thing he was supposed to say.

"Jake De Santo will stop all this! Jake De Santo will jail the teachers who are corrupting your children! Lock them up! Lock them up! For God's sake, save your children! Vote for Jake De Santo." Mallory was on such a high that he pranced around the stage several more times, waving to the cheering crowd, before he walked off to the side of the stage.

Anne led him farther off to the side, but part of the crowd followed along to cheer him on. He stopped and raised both arms in the air, evoking a cheer that for a moment drowned out Schnapps' introduction of the next speaker. He noticed that most of his excited followers were women. Anne gripped his arm, trying to pull him toward the exit. But he knew Anne was not into him, and he wanted to stay in the midst of these adoring women. They even followed him after he was down off the stage, reaching out to touch him as Anne desperately tried to pull him away. "You'll get crushed!" she screamed in his ear.

Mallory broke away from her and headed into the crowd. He wanted to feel the touch of these adoring, delirious women. He heard Anne's shriek behind him. As he turned back to her, two of the more hysterical women bumped into him and knocked him face first to the ground. He howled in pain, but then managed to gather all his courage and roll over, only to see a forest of women's legs surrounding him. One of his adoring followers was pushed from behind and fell knee first into his stomach. No one could hear his cry. A much larger woman seemed to be tottering right above his face. The irony of being crushed to death by female flesh did not escape him.

He found himself on a gurney in the parking lot. It seemed like they were about to load him into an ambulance. He realized that a one-hour stay in a hospital would cost him more than two weeks' pay. He groggily pushed himself to a sitting position and then stood up. "No hospital," he commanded the EMTs. Anne, bless her, was still there with him. "Why do they want to take me to the hospital?" he asked her.

"Just a precaution, they say. You got slammed pretty good by those women."

"I'm okay. I don't need the hospital. Will you stay with me until I catch my plane tonight?"

"That's my job."

She took him back to their hotel. He went to his room to clean up. She wasn't interested in him romantically, but he had hoped she would at least have enough maternal instinct to want to patch his scratches and clean his clothes. But no, she told him she'd meet him at the restaurant for dinner in two hours. When he looked in the mirror, he was surprised at what a large bandage the EMTs had put on the tiny scratch on his forehead. He took it off. His suit was torn, and he hadn't brought any extra clothes. But that didn't matter anyway, as all he was going to do was fly home.

Anne was nothing if not smooth. She didn't impart the bad news until he was cleaned up and sitting calmly across the table from her with a glass of cognac in his hand. "I need to tell you something. De Santo is telling his aides he didn't like the way you ran into the crowd. They're dropping you from future rallies. American Values won't be able to cover your future expenses either."

Mallory put his glass down hard, watched the liquor slosh around inside. "I guess that was a pretty short career."

"Well," she said, then waited until he raised his eyes to hers. He was curious how such a tough woman could give him such a kind look just as she was firing him. "There's another way you can look at this. That crowd absolutely loved you. They were much more excited about you than about De Santo. I think he doesn't want anyone on the rally tour who is more popular than he is. And you are outstandingly popular."

"But I'm still out of this gig."

"Yeah …. But I wouldn't worry too much about your future as an influencer. You have a way of exciting a crowd. If De Santo and American Values don't want you, there are plenty of other anti-government movements that would probably pick you up."

He didn't really believe her. He ordered another cognac and drank it slowly, savoring the taste of what would probably be the last free drink he would ever have. They fell silent. He had learned there were different kinds of relationships you could have with a woman. This was a new one.

"I should have listened to you today. You tried to warn me," he admitted.

"About that thundering herd of women?"

They shared a smile. He went on. "I guess I should have thanked you for that."

"I guess you just did." She glanced at her phone, put it down. "Your ride is coming soon." She looked up at him, sighed. "This isn't in my job description, but there's one thing I want to warn you about. You seem to be pretty easily influenced, for an influencer. I told you that all kinds of anti-government groups are going to be asking you to get on their bandwagon. Some of those groups are racist hate groups, violent people. Don't get involved with them."

He took the cab to the airport alone. He was proud to navigate his way to the gate without any help from Anne or American Values. He was held up at security because of the bruises and scabs on his face, but he stoically answered their questions and was let go. He didn't understand everything that had happened that day. He thought he would ask Spike what it all meant when he got home.

Chapter 17: An Unmanly Admission

"God, you look horrible," Kathie greeted him as she picked him up for work the next morning. "You really got trampled in Atlanta, didn't you?"

"You heard about that?"

"I saw it. They replayed it on Inside Edition. Those women looked dangerous."

"Yeah." He let out a long sigh. "They were scary. They were not my kind of women."

"Oh yeah? Who is your kind of woman? That porn star I saw on your computer?"

"Simone de Boudoir? Simone is actually a nice woman." When Kathie didn't shriek or even make a face, he decided he'd go on. "After I met her and her husband in Waco, I decided I didn't want to watch her porn show anymore."

"Oh, I see now. Simone is the ex you were talking about meeting on your last trip. You said you broke up with her. But why'd you have to go all the way to Dallas to do that?"

"Um, the breaking up came later, after …."

"You didn't! You *did* her? *On the porn site*? Are you *crazy*?"

"I was wearing a mask."

Kathie just shook her head and stared straight ahead at the road. He didn't think she had any right to be angry with him. They weren't boyfriend and girlfriend. His sex life was none of her business.

But she apparently did think it was her business. She broke the silence between them in a police interrogator's voice. "Did you pay her to fuck you?"

He had to think about that one. "Well, yes and no."

"*Yes and no*? What does *that* mean? Oh. You couldn't get it up?"

This conversation was going from bad to worse. He cringed to think about the toadstool comment she had made about his manly parts as seen in the video on his home computer. He just couldn't let her believe he had been unmanly in person with Simone. He would now have to break his vow of silence to Simone and the washing machine repairman.

"Okay. I did pay her. But we just pretended to have sex for the camera."

"What? Why would you do that? Oh, were you afraid of catching a disease or something?"

"No!" He felt insulted for Simone. "Simone doesn't have any disease. She's twenty-eight and has never had sex with anybody but her husband. I just couldn't be the first man to … you know."

"Ha! So you wasted your money."

"American Values's money."

At least she didn't lecture him. But her own romantic life was frustratingly mysterious to him. He'd been riding to work with her every day for almost two months without gaining a clue. He knew she had been into romance in the past. She had dated someone who worked at Lou's, lived for months with Rhys, even shared one passionate evening with Nell. But she didn't seem to have a current boyfriend, and all he'd ever gotten from her was that casual, thank-you hug. He worried that her single night of deviant love with Nell had somehow permanently altered her sexual organs. He tried to picture how this could have been done.

Her voice broke up his reverie. "Your speech down there in Atlanta. It was dead wrong, like from fantasyland. Those things you said about teachers were cruel. It sounded like you're not living in the real world anymore."

"You're just brainwashed by the elite media propaganda." It suddenly hit him that maybe that was the reason she was keeping him at a distance. "It's really a shame that an intelligent person like you can't see the truth."

"You realize you're calling me stupid, don't you?"

"Maybe you know a lot about statistics, but you don't know anything about life. Nobody with any common sense would hang around with – live with – that creep, Rhys."

"Oh, that's what this is about. You're jealous."

He didn't know what to say. They went into the UniCast building without speaking again. That afternoon, she drove him to his second job at Lou's as usual, but they didn't speak then either. They didn't speak for the next two days, even as she picked him up and drove him to both jobs like clockwork. Mallory sat in her passenger seat in utter silence. He knew it was idiotic. He craved some kind of conversation with her, but he didn't know how to start it.

He met Spike on Saturday, expecting the worst. Spike told him that half their sponsors, almost all of those associated with American Values, had dropped their ads. "What's worse," he told Mallory now, "is that our likes and followers seemed to have peaked. We haven't gained any new followers this week."

"So? Is that it? Are we over?"

"You don't seem to be that upset." Spike himself looked really upset. He seemed even more upset when his father then interrupted their meeting to remind him to wait on customers sitting in two booths in the back. Rolling his eyes at his father's comment, Spike stormed out the front door of the Dough and Go and stood outside, hands on hips, staring up at the sky like he was daring God to strike him down, or strike somebody down. But then, after just a minute, he turned back and politely approached the other waiting diners. Mallory finished his burger quickly and left.

By the following Saturday, however, Spike had changed his tune completely. The gleam was back in his eyes as he practically ran toward Mallory's booth.

"Nothing gets up more interest than a counterattack," he crowed. He slid his phone toward Mallory. "Here's what I posted a few days ago."

DE SANTO ORDERS MOB OF HARRIDAN FOLLOWERS TO TRAMPLE EDUCATION INFLUENCER! Kevin Mallory, whose heartfelt speech condemning teachers for indoctrinating our children was met with widespread approval at a De Santo rally in Atlanta, was later viciously attacked by a hand-picked coterie of thugs. De Santo ordered the attack when he saw that Mallory's growing popularity threatened to overshadow his own quest for the presidency.

"De Santo ordered that?" Mallory was dumbfounded.

"Look. Look here at the clip." Mallory winced at the video of him being crushed under the crowd of screaming females.

"But it wasn't an attack. They liked me. They were screaming my name."

"*Details. Details.* They almost killed you. And the important thing is, your overall following, which had started to slip as soon as American Values dropped you, firmed up within an hour after this was posted. And your accusation that De Santo ordered that beating made the *Washington Post* and *The New York Times*."

"Will I get any money soon?"

"We're a little low right now. The ad revenue hasn't bounced back yet. And I had to pay some guys. The Cat-A-Tonic people were our biggest advertiser, and they're gone. I do have a plan to get them back soon. But right now, I think I can get you another $150. I'll bring it around to your apartment sometime next week."

*** ***

"I hate you!" Nell didn't hit him or knock over his coffee this time. She didn't threaten to sue him. She just plopped herself down in the chair that was squeezed between his desk and the cubicle wall. "Why are you doing the *Nell* thing again? The *Nell Chronicles*, for God's sake! A whole website devoted to poisoning everyone's mind against me?"

"Oh. I didn't know. I guess Spike's doing that again."

"There's nothing I can do about it, is there?" Her eyes were red. Her hair had long since grown out of its neat bob and was now even falling out of its imprisonment in those tortoiseshell barrettes.

"Spike wants to monetize our social media stuff, but the Cat-A-Tonic people have cancelled their ads. He said we can't get them back without the *Nell* thing."

"You don't understand. My neighbors won't even talk to me anymore. And when they think I'm not home, they sneak around my yard to make sure my cats and dogs aren't being experimented on – like you're saying on X I'm doing. A guy at the grocery store last night asked me if all gay people torture animals."

Mallory felt sorry for her. Enough time had passed since they had directly done each other harm. And he had no reason to feel superior to her. She had failed with Kathie because Kathie wasn't gay, while he had no excuse for why he was failing with Kathie. Spike was bringing back *Nell*, and there didn't seem to be any way to stop him.

"Maybe you should change your name."

She burst into tears. He took a Dough and Go napkin from his bag of snacks on his desk and handed it to her. She wiped her eyes and blew her nose, but she kept crying. He hesitated, then pulled out the last Dough and Go napkin and handed it to her.

"Thank you." Her voice was as subdued as he'd ever heard it. "I did. I thought about changing my name, but why should I have to, and what good would that do anyway?"

Mallory had no idea. He was not used to figuring out other people's problems.

"You know," she went on, confessing. "The Kathie thing was hard on me. Then Koko died. And now people avoid me everywhere, even my old friends. If I get near the little kids in the neighborhood, their parents come out and drag them back inside."

"Maybe you should go back to Healing Hearts."

"Oh sure. Right. You want me to go back there and argue with Mr. *Ramsteel* again."

Chapter 18: Cat-A-Tonic

"It's working!" Spike was ecstatic. "Our numbers are going up again. There's memes and videos everywhere trashing De Santo for being too scared to take on the school system like you did. I don't think anybody really believes he sicced that mob of witches on you on purpose, but my post got everybody's attention."

"But can we stop with the *Nell* stuff?"

"That's the other good part. After I got back into *Nell*, the number of followers immediately picked up again, and that got the Cat-A-Tonic people back. They've contracted for another 90 days at least. Paid ads, in advance."

"You promised you would stop the *Nell* stuff."

"We're committed to Cat-A-Tonic. If we stop now, we can be sued."

"I don't care." Mallory had nothing, so he had nothing to lose in a lawsuit.

"But what if they sue *me*?" There was a tinge of fear in Spike's voice that Mallory had never noticed before. "And what about my father? He's spent his whole life building up the Dough and Go. A lawsuit could take that all away in a second."

Mallory didn't see how the Dough and Go could be involved in a lawsuit. But he knew this discussion was way over his head. His many adventures in court hadn't taught him a thing about the law. But this lawsuit talk made him worried for Spike's father. Would he and Spike ultimately have to choose between driving Nell to despair or taking the Dough and Go from the old man?

He had recently noticed that Spike was acting a little erratically. Manic Mallory was making up more and more outlandish lies. Spike had promised to lay off Nell, but now he was doubling down on her. And Mallory also wondered why he had earned only $300 from all of Spike's efforts, and why internet-savvy Spike, of all people, would

115

pay him in cash.

"Stop this *Nell* business. Somebody's going to get hurt somehow. I don't want to be any part of it."

Spike's eyes narrowed. "No way! I've created a juggernaut here, no thanks to you. And if it goes down, I'm back slinging burgers. That's never gonna happen."

*** ***

Mallory was surprised when Harrison called him into his office to talk, alone. The supervisor still didn't have the latest upgraded computer on his desk. He still looked disheveled. As soon as Mallory sat down, Harrison shocked him again by pulling a bottle out of a desk drawer and offering him a drink. He poured and, strangely, they found themselves toasting each other with tiny shot glasses of cognac.

"I never used to drink cognac," Harrison started. "But I keep hearing employees talking about it. Not bad, huh?"

"Yeah, I like cognac." He thought he'd give Harrison a tip. "Women like it, too."

"Yeah, I think that's where I heard about it from. I think it was Nell."

Mallory was quite familiar with Nell's drinking. She had pretty much gotten smashed every time he had been out with her. Now that he was no longer trying to seduce her, he noticed that her drinking was probably a bad thing. He didn't have the nerve to say this to her in person, but he wondered if the people in Healing Hearts would bring this out in her, if she ever went back to that therapy group.

"You ruined my career here." Harrison rocked back in his chair, strangely smiling, as if he didn't really care about his career at UniCast anymore. "The Miss Marcie affair put a black mark on my record that UniCast will never forget. But, in retrospect …."

Harrison stopped and smiled to himself as if he were proud he could use such a big word in his condition. "In retrospect, I was the one who started it. It was cruel of me to threaten to fire her for coming in four hours late. The poor woman had a flat tire. I deserved all the humiliation I got."

"They're firing you? Why are you telling me this? Are you saying you want to hire me to defend you?"

Harrison laughed, poured another half shot for himself and Mallory. "No, no. They haven't fired me, not yet. But I have no future here. And I might have another position lined up. You might not believe this, but I had a pretty decent career going before I came here."

Mallory had no concept of what a pretty decent career might be. And he didn't understand why Harrison would quit just because the company was trying to get rid of him. He thought that was pretty normal. His own employers had always been trying to get rid of him.

"Anyway, as you know, UniCast ordered me to fire you, but Ms. Marcie and I are stalling on getting the paperwork done. I've told them I have to move extremely carefully now because of your status as an influencer." Harrison smirked at that title. "Bottom line, I'm pretty sure you can keep your job at UniCast as long as you want."

*** ***

Kathie didn't have to think for a second after he told her what Harrison had said. "Keep your job at Lou's. I'm no lawyer, but I think UniCast has a good case against you. It was an outright lie to say that they refused you a promotion when you didn't even apply for one."

"Spike made up that *promotion* crap. He said what actually happened was just a *detail*. Not the important part. The important part is UniCast is screwing all its employees."

"Uhhn! Now I understand why you can't keep a girlfriend, or a job, for very long. Kevin, listen. A lie, is a lie, is a lie."

"You're lying about my customer approval ratings."

Kathie put the tips of her fingers to her face, as she sometimes did when something had caught her up. "Okay. You're right. Starting tomorrow, I'm putting the accurate customer approval ratings in your file."

"You know I can't get fired for that anyway, now. Harrison's going to keep me as long as he's here."

"Good. Good all around."

She dropped him off at Lou's. Mallory hadn't admitted to her that he was having a difficult time fitting in at that dealership. The customers seemed to be making up problems, even when their perfectly new cars were in perfect condition. At least, that's what the mechanics told him after they'd spent a lot of their time trying to identify some shadowy noise or vibration or shudder that the customers claimed were driving them crazy. Fortunately, even these new cars seemed to be always in need of a fluid change of some sort, or a wiper replacement at the least, and so the time spent chasing the phantom problem wasn't totally wasted. And he was amazed at how stupid some of the customers were. They would come in complaining that the car was dripping brake fluid but not even notice that the car needed four new tires until after Mallory handed them the bill. He parroted to the customers whatever the mechanics told him. But when he told one woman customer that her belt tensioner was not doing the job, she said she was going to report him for sexual harassment.

He was trying to get some advice from Rick, his supervisor, when Lou, the owner of the dealership, walked by the open door to that office. Lou walked in and edged himself between Mallory's chair and Rick's desk, stopping their conversation. Eyes wide in apparent shock, he leaned down, gently touched Mallory's jaw and turned it slowly left to right, right to left, inspecting the bruises and scratches on his face like a concerned surgeon. "You're a wounded warrior, *our* wounded warrior."

"I'm a Martyr of God," Mallory replied reflexively.

"Damn straight! Damn government's running roughshod over us regular folk. And now they're using our teachers to go after our children. I had no idea that was happening right here in our county. You're a hero to all of us regular hardworking people." He turned to Rick. "Be good to this man." He left without waiting for a response.

Rick seemed annoyed. He leaned back in his squeaky rotating chair. "What were we talking about? Oh yeah. Why only women customers need brake fluid and antifreeze flushes. Well, the way we work here at Lou's …."

"I get it. I get it." Mallory was proud to have figured out the answer all by himself. "It's something about the way their bodies are different, the different way their bodies use fluids and all."

When Mallory saw Rick's jaw drop open, he knew he had surprised his manager with his worldly wisdom. Rick seemed hesitant to look Mallory in the eye for a moment. But then he nodded in agreement. "Yes. Very perceptive of you, Mr. Mallory. But remember that there are exceptions. Sometimes, the mechanics may tell you that a man's car needs a brake flush, too. This can happen sometimes, and there's nothing wrong with that."

"Oh. Okay. Is that all for now? They're calling for me back in the shop."

"One more thing. It can sometimes happen in the opposite way. Like, for example, if you get any women *attorney* customers, they don't need flushes."

Chapter 19: Whose Company?

"Hello, this is Kevin Mallory at the UniCast Cable customer assistance line. How may I help you?"

"Mr. Mallory, this is not a customer. This is Anne from American Values. I know I should have called you sooner to ask how you're recovering from that incident at the Atlanta rally."

"Um, I'm okay." He didn't know what else to say. He had no experience with anyone ever calling him to ask how he was.

There was a long silence on the line before Anne went on. "Mr. Mallory, I have really important news for you. Senator De Santo is apparently getting a lot of criticism from the right for banning you from his rallies. There are a lot of people who want you back."

"I'm not going anywhere near that crowd of women."

"But listen, please. De Santo has contacted American Values. He wants you back. He wants you onstage with him. You'd be totally protected from those women. De Santo now says he loved the talk you gave about teachers encouraging children to experiment with their sexual identities. Especially your Play Doh comment."

"Would I get money for this?"

"If you agree to a short tour – three rallies – American Values will pay all your expenses. And it gets even better. The De Santo campaign will pay you $500 per appearance."

"Sign me up."

*** ***

Mallory was furious that Spike was still making up elaborate lies about Nell just to incite the cat lovers of the world. "You don't listen to anything I say. Nell is furious. Sometimes she's crying. There's no telling what she'll do."

Spike waved his hand as if brushing away a fly. "That cat thing is where most of the money for our company is coming from."

"I didn't even know we had a company."

"I had to set up a company bank account to cash the Cat-A-Tonic checks."

"How much money do we have?"

"We have ... a little. I'm having to pay some geeks I knew from school to keep Manic Mallory updated. Between us all, we're posting something new, somewhere, every half hour, twenty-four-seven. You're a hero. That's why De Santo caved in. He's terrified you'll turn against him."

Mallory had thought the strange feeling in his stomach came from the green salads he was now ordering in his quest to keep Kathie off his back about his diet. But now he knew that queasy feeling was coming from Spike. And Spike's next idea made his digestion worse.

"By the way, make sure the De Santo campaign makes out the checks to our company."

"Wait a minute. Anne told me De Santo was giving the money to *me*. I'm keeping that money. If I ever get it."

"Oh, you'll get it for sure. De Santo is running scared of our followers. But you need to deposit that money in our company's account."

Chapter 20: Money for Nothing, Chick for Free

Mallory bounced onto the stage as the theme from *Rocky* hyped the audience. The crowd went wild as he circled the stage three times, pumping his fists to the music. Anne had told him that the De Santo people wanted him to be the attack dog and to show no mercy to the forces corrupting the youth of the country. But she told him also he had to say at least a word or two about the positive values Dr Santo and his people stood for. She had handed him some written notes as they lunched in the hotel dining room over drinks. He liked looking at Anne, and he liked dealing with her, too. He made sure she saw him glancing at her notes.

"Do you like your job?" he surprised himself by asking.

She delivered her answer to his question with a little smirk. "It pays well. I get to travel a lot, but that's getting old. The people running American Values are smart, and my immediate boss has a good sense of humor, but …."

She had nearly reached the limit of Mallory's attention span when it came to listening to other people's stories. But lately he had begun to realize that not much was happening in his own life, and he might as well listen to what people were thinking – at least what hot women like Anne were thinking. "But what?"

"American Values is a creation of the offshore oil industry. Their whole reason for their existence is to elect politicians who will cut taxes on offshore oil drilling operations."

"What about the children, and the teachers, and the LGBTQ-plusses?"

"The only thing that American Values cares about is offshore drilling taxes."

Mallory realized Anne was a type of creature he had never run into before: a smart, hot young woman who made a lot of money and traveled all over the country meeting all kinds of important people – but who was unhappy. It wasn't unusual for the women he was with to say they were unhappy. It usually meant they wanted to be taken to a different restaurant, or wanted him to come up with better conversation, or better drinks, or they wanted to be taken home. Once in a great while, and not at all in the last year or so, it meant they wanted to be taken to bed. But he had no idea now what Anne meant.

"You need something else in your life?" He was not trying to flirt. He had long ago given up on the idea of attracting this classy woman – or any classy woman, for that matter. He meant to ask this as the most bland, open-ended question possible.

"Not what you're thinking." She smiled ruefully. Mallory was pleased that she had even imagined he was trying to flirt with her. "I'm not sure what I want, exactly. I'm putting all my energy into this job right now, but I just have this feeling that I need to do something better with my life."

They finished their lunch in silence, but Anne perked up on the way to the rally, prodding him with ideas about his speech. He only pretended to listen. He was much more interested in how the crowd would react. And he was not disappointed. As he paraded himself around the stage in sync with the Manic Mallory character on the giant screen behind him, the crowd roared. When he finally stopped and stepped toward the microphone, the roars grew even louder. He felt he had finally found the place where he belonged.

"I'm back! The people have spoken. Even the mighty De Santo now recognizes my genius. But you recognized it first, you put me in your hearts. I thank you all from the bottom of my own heart." The crowd's excitement penetrated and inspired him. He had been allotted fifteen minutes to speak. He still had no idea what he was going to say.

He decided to let the crowd tell him what they wanted. "Free our kids! Free our kids! Free our kids!" they shouted. When he echoed them, the crowd roared again. He waited, but they didn't come up with anything else, so he had to think of something on his own. He was glad he had listened to *God's Truth* on the plane.

"The Indoctrinators – that's what I call our WOKE teachers – the Indoctrinators say they want to be inclusive. Inclusive of what? I'll tell you what. They want to be inclusive of sodomy, of bestiality, of sex operations on kindergarteners, of copulation with animals, of forced transgender operations." The crowd roared its disapproval of each of these subjects, which were apparently being taught in schools throughout the country.

"But it gets even worse. God's Martyrs has now unearthed an even more sickening plot to use our children's DNA to transform our country into something never seen on earth before. They are milking our older children for eggs and sperm, in school, so every child in the next generation will be born an orphan in a test tube, an orphan with no real parents, with no idea of who they are. We can't let this happen in America!"

While the crowd let out low groans of disapproval, he took a moment to look for any attractive women in the front rows who might be interested in more than listening to his speech. Other than Anne and a few glamorous De Santo aides, none of whom seemed to be paying any attention to his speech, he saw no one in the crowd he would risk being trampled for.

"This newly-discovered plot is designed to create a whole new generation of anonymous orphans, with no connection to any real parents, or to God. They will be rootless, heartless zombies, groomed to take over our country. And destroy everything you, their parents, ever cherished or loved. It will be *Children of the School*, a worse horror movie than *Children of the Corn*." He stepped back, but the crowd didn't immediately react, so he repeated the phrase, using the voice of an old ad for that old, scary movie, pumping his fist wildly. "*Children of the School!*"

The crowd got the idea and took up the chant: "*Children of the School, Children of the School.*"

He glanced back at Anne, who was tapping on her cell phone. He wished he had brought the speech she had written for him, or at least looked at it, because he didn't have anything else to say. He had studied a lot more material on *God's Truth*, especially those insightful analyses of how LGBT-plusses and WOKES were pushing ordinary people like him to the back of the line. But he hadn't been studying those particular truths as much lately. He'd been too busy working at Lou's and arguing with Spike and fending off Nell's hatred and pining for a closer connection with Kathie. Besides, with the money now pouring in from American Values, he felt like he was now beating the LGBTQ+ at their own game.

He decided to repeat his prance around the stage. He tried to signal the technical people to play the *Rocky* theme. When that didn't happen, he decided to perform anyway, syncopating his movements with *Children of the School* chant still going on. When that started to die out, he turned his back on the audience and wiggled his rear end to the beat of the fading chant. This brought a huge round of laughter. But he thought better of that tactic. He remembered that he was obligated to mention De Santo and say that he would be the savior of the country. He walked back to the mike, held his hand up for silence, and delivered the minimum required words of praise for the presidential candidate.

"They loved it," Anne said drily as they met afterward in the hotel restaurant for dinner.

"You didn't?"

"It was a little schlocky for me. But it served its purpose. Nobody gets that crowd as excited as you do. And the media can't keep their cameras off you. I'm going to check the latest polling, but I wouldn't be surprised if you've become as popular as De Santo himself now."

*** ***

The first thing he did when he got the check from the De Santo campaign was ask Kathie out on a date. They were in her truck outside of Lou's Lexus. He had been in contact with her most of the day, but he didn't get up the nerve until she was about to let him off.

She froze up the second he asked her.

Had he just lost the only person outside of the internet world who regularly talked to him? The person who was still was driving him to both jobs?

"You don't have to say anything," he said quickly as he reached for the door handle.

"No. Wait." Her voice was loud, almost panicky. "If you have the nerve to do it, so do I."

Five hundred dollars wasn't enough to buy a car, so of course she had to drive. He hoped she wouldn't whore herself up like most women did on dates. It wasn't that he didn't like the whorish look; it just didn't seem like that would be the real Kathie. She did wear long silver earrings that intermittently flashed behind her curls. Her pale blue jeans looked new. He would have been happy with a burger in a bar, but the Maryland summer seemed to be holding out until October, and she wanted to go to a free concert she'd heard about in a county park. They sat at a picnic table and watched a young, earnest folk-rock trio featuring a pretty girl singer and two grinning, handsome guys on guitar and bass. Mallory didn't generally like the egos of the performers he'd seen on YouTube, but these guys were so obviously happy to play, and so unpretentious, that he let down his guard. When the band went on a break, he walked up and talked to them. He knew nothing about music, so he started asking them about their amplifiers. The two guys, especially, seemed happy to talk about their sound system. Mallory wasn't used to having any conversation that wasn't a confrontation, or having anything at all to say, and this interlude was so pleasant he stayed up near the stage with them until he noticed Kathie looking worried.

"The amplifiers," he began. "They're the same brand they were using in Atlanta," he informed her. "Only the ones in Atlanta were a lot bigger."

"I don't want to talk about Atlanta, or your other life. You know I think that's all demented."

Mallory did what he had to do. He erased from his mind any thought of Atlanta, or De Santo, or Anne, or Spike, or American Values, or even amplifiers. He pondered what was left to talk about. But she already knew everything about his jobs at UniCast and Lou's, and she had already seen his newly cleaned apartment. There was only one thing left to talk about. Her.

"Is one of the guys in the band your ex-boyfriend?"

"No. Why would you say that?"

"I don't know. You wanted to come here. You must have a lot of exes. Every guy seems to like you."

"Oh, you're so wrong about me. My girlfriends tell me I don't even know how to dress. And I'm five-foot-eight. I think you're the first man under six feet who ever dared look me in the eye and talk to me."

"But you had boyfriends. You had Rhys."

He expected her to answer that Rhys was six feet two, but she just sighed and went quiet. But when he didn't say anything else, she went on. "I guess I can tell you, Kevin. Rhys was kind of a desperation move on my part. But I learned something about myself from that affair. I really did."

He didn't have the nerve to ask her what she learned from another man. "I don't see it. Everyone loves you. Even that lezzie, Nell, fell in love with you."

"Nell! God! Talk about desperation."

Mallory had never noticed any sign of desperation in Kathie. But he realized now that he had never looked past those startling green eyes, that long, voluptuous body, and that glorious crown of curls. He was shocked when he realized she was now telling him she sometimes felt like a dork.

"Desperation? You? Desperate? That's impossible."

"I know what you think. You think men like me because of my

looks. But you don't know how many of my romances have ended after the first date."

Mallory was stunned. He couldn't see anything wrong with Kathie at all. He couldn't fathom why any man would lose interest in her. But then he started worrying. Was this just her way of telling him that their first date would be their last? He started to prepare himself for that. Fortunately, he was used to rejection.

Kathie was only person he talked to all week besides Spike. He didn't want to lose that. But he would lose that if this date ended in disaster. He realized that most men would now try to save the day by telling her how beautiful she was. Manly Man recommended that phrase for almost every occasion. Besides, he did think she was beautiful. But he didn't trust either his instincts or Manly Man anymore. He was lost. But he wanted to know more about her anyway.

They stayed after the concert and had a drink from a flask that they had sneaked in. They sat on the picnic bench together, watching the violet twilight through the trees as the crowd slowly thinned out. With so much of his life a forbidden subject between them, he had no choice but to keep asking her about hers. She told him she had graduated from college and driven around the country with a girlfriend, camping in a tent. That friend lived in Chicago now, and she rarely heard from her. Her mother had died while she was in college. Her father lived in Texas now, and she had a "so-so" relationship with him. A few of her girlfriends at work had shut her down after she had dumped Nell. "I guess that makes me scary to them, from a lot of perspectives," she laughed.

He wondered how she could laugh at losing some of her work friends through no fault of her own. At this point, he knew he had reached the limit of how much time he could usually spend listening to another person's problems. But he felt he needed to make an exception now for her. He needed to know more about something she'd mentioned before.

"You told me you really bonded with your brother and sister in Mexico. Cried and all. What was that all about?"

"That was right after I broke up with Rhys," she sighed. "I'll tell you the whole story if you want to hear it." She gave him a chance to object, then went on. "I mean, he was a complete mess. Our apartment looked like a giant man cave. He wouldn't eat anything I made. He'd go out and never tell me when he was coming back.

"People always tell me I'm too rigid. So I made an effort to adjust to his ways. I really tried. And I thought it was working. Then last summer we were going to go to Mexico to meet my brother and sister on vacation. But, at the last minute, he didn't go. That's another long story. I flew down there myself, crying all the way. My sister said my whole way of thinking about men was wrong. You can't change yourself just to hold onto someone who's drifting away."

"Oh." Mallory's voice was flat because he was mentally salivating over the image of Kathie lying on the beach next to him for a week in Mexico. "What an idiot. Rhys, I mean."

"Thanks for listening to my sob story." She snorted a laugh at her own description. "There are not really a lot of people who talk to me. Tell me something about yourself. Except nothing about politics, or God's Martyrs."

"Okay, um, at work, there's a mechanic who sometimes puts my work at the bottom of the pile," Mallory contributed. He was glad his experiences at Lou's were not a taboo subject between him and Kathie. But after he said this, she suddenly went silent and looked away from him and up toward the violet sky. "Does it bother you when I talk about Lou's?" he asked.

"No. No. We can talk about Lou's. Of course," she said, but she was staring up at the purplish clouds as if she didn't want to meet his eyes. "Okay." She finally brought her eyes down from those clouds. "I told you I used to date someone who worked at Lou's. It didn't end well. I had to break up with him. Then he started calling me and texting me – for the next two years. He was kind of obsessed. I finally had to ghost him. His name is Victor."

Mallory now realized why Victor had held up the brake job on Ms. Thomasson's car. He was jealous of Mallory's friendship with

Kathie. But before he could tell her about that strange incident, she floored him with a statement he didn't see coming. "Victor is the only reason I've never come in to see you working at Lou's."

"You wanted to see me at work?" Mallory was stunned. No one had ever before expressed any interest in seeing him at his work.

"Sure. I've been curious to see you in your new situation there."

"I didn't know people did that."

"I didn't say everybody does that. I just said I wanted to see you there."

Mallory imagined her being with him at Lou's, maybe standing with him at his little stand, maybe all day. He knew that would have made him nervous, at first. He would have wanted to ask her to explain things to him – but out of pride, he wouldn't have asked her for any advice. He would have gradually figured out the job for himself, just as he was doing now. Yes, he had performed his job at Lou's just as she would have wanted him to. It was almost as if she had always been there with him, almost as if he had never been alone there.

Mallory knew that Rhys was still bitter about their breakup. He wondered now about Victor. "Do you think Victor's still obsessed with you, after all this time?" She didn't answer, but he decided such a thing could easily happen. He doubted that any man who ever loved her could ever forget her.

It seemed now like the whole world was suffused with Kathie's presence. She had somehow traveled back in time and retroactively sanctioned all of that he had done at Lou's. And he wasn't the only one she affected. Everywhere he turned, she was there, being loved or hated, spurned or needed, castigated or lusted after. She was everywhere, always, like a local goddess he hadn't had the sense to worship yet. He inched nearer to her on the picnic bench. It was embarrassing that she was still taller than him, even sitting down. But he dared to touch her arm and move closer. He was trying to conquer his fear. Then she pulled him to her and suddenly kissed him, seemingly as eager and nervous as he was. They breathed together in shock at their sudden communion. He wished they weren't in public. But where else would you find a goddess?

Chapter 21: Eat the Brakes

Lou ordered Rick Gunther to pay Mallory for all the time he missed while stumping for De Santo on the campaign trail. This didn't help Rick's mood. He told Mallory he had to make up for the time lost by "selling, selling, selling." Mallory was determined to make a go of this job, and he was happy to get Rick's advice on how to sell.

One of the first things he learned was that nobody needed just front brakes. No matter what the specifications for brake pad thickness were, he was to tell customers they needed brakes "all around." He didn't know what this phrase meant, and he didn't like the questioning looks some of the mechanics gave him, but most of the customers were appreciative when they learned of this additional dangerous condition. But one customer, a crusty old man, insisted on talking to the mechanic himself.

"He's not here," Mallory explained on the phone. "The mechanics are all gone. They work on the day shift."

"Then I'll be in tomorrow morning."

Mallory could sense trouble coming, so he thought he'd try to head it off right then. "If you don't get back brakes, they will overcompensate for the new front brakes and fall off."

"I spent twenty years as a diesel mechanic, and I never heard of such a thing."

"Well, these cars are not diesels." Mallory was pretty sure that was true.

"Give me your manager's phone number, right now."

"I don't know his phone number." Mallory had a sudden fear that the man would come in right then and quiz him about the brakes, about which he knew nothing. "But he'll definitely be in tomorrow morning. If you want, I'll leave a message on his desk that you want to speak to him."

Mallory Meets His Match

Rick was waiting for him, hands on hips, when Mallory showed up for work the next afternoon. "Your customer, *the diesel mechanic*, came in to see me this morning. What kind of cockamamie story did you tell him about the brakes falling off?"

"You told me everybody needs rear brakes. He asked me why. I didn't know exactly why, so I just had to kind of guess."

"You don't know anything at all about cars, do you?"

Mallory searched in vain for an answer that would allow him to keep his job, but then he gave up. "No."

Rick motioned for him to follow him into the office. "You're lucky the mechanic got a good look at that guy when he dropped the car off. Otherwise, we'd have to eat those rear brakes."

Mallory was completely confounded by Rick's statement: *eat those rear brakes*. And what difference did it make that the mechanic had looked at the customer? He wondered for a second if Rick was on drugs, but he didn't dare say anything like that.

"Didn't you tell me everybody needed rear brakes?"

Rick located a pencil somewhere under his computer monitor and put it in his mouth and manipulated it as if he wished it were a cigarette. He sat back and held Mallory's eyes before he spoke. "I can't get rid of you because Lou thinks you're going to save the country. Okay. Listen. Yes, almost everybody who gets front brakes needs rear brakes. But, not diesel mechanics, not old men, not women lawyers, not anyone who's had new rear brakes within the last year. If they ask you why they need 'em, there's only one answer: the pads are less than a sixteenth of an inch and they'll damage the rotors if they aren't immediately replaced."

Mallory complained to Kathie on the way home. "This job is a lot harder than I thought it would be."

"Oh, yeah? Why's that?"

"I don't know. There's a lot more people involved. Sometimes one person says one thing and another says another. But, no matter what, there's a real customer who can yell right in my face if something goes wrong."

"It's harder than Customer Assistance at UniCast Cable?"

"A lot harder. You can't click anybody off. The customers know my real name. I can't understand half of what the mechanics are saying, but I have to sound like I know what I'm doing. I make promises to the customers about when their cars will be ready, but sometimes the parts come in when they're supposed to, sometimes they don't."

"I guess all jobs have their problems, and hassles. I guess that's why they pay people to do them."

*** ***

She hadn't come in when she dropped him off from their date in the park. He had been thinking about her too much to keep up a conversation. The local world of UniCast and Lou's and Kathie outshone all his internet ambitions. He wanted to know even more about her, but the frisson he felt from her kiss had been so strong he could hardly speak.

Chapter 22: Eggs, Sperm and Dog Food

Mallory saw a man wrestling with the UniCast security guard just outside his cubicle. Terrified of any type of physical confrontation, he jumped out of his chair and tried to make himself invisible behind the partition. The sound of the commotion continued with low-volume rustling and grunting until Nell came out of the next cubicle and screamed at the men to stop.

"I'm with the Associated Press," the man explained, as much to Nell as to the security guard. "We have permission from UniCast to interview an employee who works here, Kevin Mallory. I'm just trying to do my job. Please talk to your manager."

The security guard checked the man's ID, then walked off, telling him not to move until he came back. Nell appeared at Mallory's cubicle entrance, leaned in, and hissed. "It's a reporter. I swear, Mallory, if you say a word about the *Nell* thing, or if you tell him I am the original Nell, I will make you pay, if it's the last thing I do."

The reporter, listening in, caught on that he was at the right cubicle. "Mr. Mallory, I would like to talk to you about your amazing, sudden political ascendancy. If you come outside, maybe we can talk in private. I can guarantee you the whole world wants to hear your opinions." Mallory was pleased to follow him out.

"First of all, I'd like your reaction to the fact that, according to our most recent poll, you are more popular than Jake De Santo, the leading candidate in the primary race for President of the United States."

"What?"

The reporter explained that Mallory's approval rating was higher than that of De Santo. Mallory's rating was 31%, while De Santo's was 23%.

"What's 'approval rating?'"

The reporter paused. "It means overall approval, taking everything into consideration: your policies, your background, your charisma, and I guess in your case including the popularity of your cartoon image, Manic Mallory, the one with the goatee and the beads."

"I don't wear a goatee anymore."

"Of course. I can see that. But the important news here is you are more popular than De Santo. What do you attribute that popularity to?"

"I guess it's because I'm exposing the truth about how teachers are indoctrinating our kids."

"You have said that the public schools are harvesting the children's sperm and eggs to raise a race of anonymous zombies. Where did you get that information from?"

"Don't you get it? That information is out there, everywhere. The mainstream media, all they talk about is the gays and WOKES and LGBTQ-plusses. 'Praise be to the deviants,' they say. They ignore the real truth. *The Real Honest to God's Truth*. Where else would I get the truth?"

"That website is your only source of information?"

"I'm an official member of God's Martyrs. We know what we know."

"You posted that the UniCast Corporation failed to hire you for a position because of your race."

"That's confidential. They said they'd sue me if I talked about it anymore."

"So, are you saying it's an ongoing dispute?"

"I'm not saying anything. End of interview." He ran inside and hid in the break room. He kept away from his cubicle the rest of the day. He tried to call Spike, but his young mentor didn't pick up. He was so flustered and excited by the interview that he couldn't even focus on Kathie when she drove him to Lou's after work. He'd promised her he would keep his internet life separate from her, but it was hard not to tell her about this exciting news. It was hard not to ask her advice. But he thought it best to say nothing.

Kathie didn't mention their night at the concert. He was afraid that meant he was just another one of her failed, one-time dates. But she *had* kissed him that night. He had longed for the touch of her lips for so long, he had been deliriously lost in them. He had tried to keep their communion going while disciplining himself not to be too greedy. But, after what seemed to him like just a minute, she had gently pushed him away. He thought she might be embarrassed to be kissing in a public park. Or maybe she was embarrassed because she was kissing *him*. He had no idea, and no idea how to find out. For all he knew, a kiss was just something she thought she had to do on any date, just to get it over with.

But she hardly talked to him at all the next day until they were in the truck and almost at Lou's. "I'm not talking," she finally announced. "Because I'm so pissed."

"I thought you wanted me to kiss you."

"Jesus Christ! Not that! I was following you on X late last night. I just can't understand why you would say those awful things about teachers. I'm starting to think something really bad might have happened to you as a kid, in school."

"Nothing good ever happened to me in school."

"Are you saying you were sexually abused?" She hesitated. "I feel like we're getting a little bit closer now, Kevin. We can talk about stuff like this, I hope. Don't you think?"

"Um, I guess so."

"Do you think you can trust me a little now? Will you tell me if you were abused as a child? By a teacher? I want to know, and I want to help you. Nothing you tell me will shock me."

For a moment he wished he had been abused by a teacher.

"It was horrible. I can't say anything."

"Oh, Kevin, I'm so sorry."

He didn't know why he let the conversation end like that. He had never been sexually abused by any teacher, or even by his parents. But in therapy he had learned there were different kinds of abuse. He had learned that constantly being ignored by his father and called an imbecile by his mother was a kind of abuse. He felt he deserved Kathie's pity, even if only for that. He had promised himself never to lie to her, but this wasn't a lie. He had been abused.

*** ***

Huddled in the corner booth at the Dough and Go, Mallory and Spike took what was supposed to be an important call from Anne.

"De Santo is sinking in the polls," she started right away, not even saying hello. "American Values is really worried. They've put their money on him, and he's going nowhere. But there's a big segment of the public that loves you, Kevin. My idea is to shore up De Santo by putting you on the ticket."

"What's a ticket?"

Spike put his hand over Mallory's mouth and said quickly. "We understand. American Values wants Mr. Mallory to run for vice-president with De Santo."

"Yes. American Values wants it to happen. And De Santo is pretty much in their pocket."

"We agree!" Spike shouted, his eyes for once showing a happy glow. "Mallory for vice president! It'll be tweeted out within 60 seconds."

"Um, you might want to wait on that. What I just told you is that American Values wants it to happen. De Santo hasn't agreed yet."

"We'll make him agree."

They could hear Anne's sigh over the phone. "Suit yourself. What I have to do is tell American Values that Mr. Mallory agrees. Can I assume from our conversation that he agrees?"

"He agrees," Spike snapped back.

"What does it mean?" Mallory asked after they hung up.

"It means De Santo is desperate. Nobody picks a vice presidential candidate before the primaries have even started. He's desperate for your help."

"What does it mean for me?"

"Are you kidding? It means your life spent scrabbling for pennies is over. It means you'll travel all over the country on De Santo's dime. It means you are a full-fledged influencer who can command hundreds if not thousands of dollars each time you mention a product."

"Okay. Sounds good. Are we rich enough that we can drop the Cat-A-Tonic people?" He was still bitter that Spike had never listened to him and had never let up on Nell.

"I have no control over that anymore. I had to turn over the advertising end to a marketing firm, Influence Peddlers, Inc. They do the contracts. Some dog food people signed on, too. I don't know exactly what for."

Chapter 23: Minus One More

Nell looked awful. She'd let her hair grow long again, and she wasn't even putting it up in those barrettes anymore. Whenever he walked by and glanced in her cubicle, she seemed like she had shrunk even more. Mallory felt the opposite. He felt he was on the verge of getting all the fame and power and romance he'd always known he deserved. Mallory's memory of the slights he had suffered was almost as short as his memory of the humiliations he had heaped on others. He could hardly remember why he and Nell were supposed to hate each other. He stopped one morning to try to cheer her up.

"There's only three members of my Cheer Committee left," she answered his inquiry bitterly. "People won't look me in the eye. You've got me branded as an animal torturer. My neighbors are staring at my house with binoculars. Some anonymous person reported me to Animal Control. How am I supposed to feel?"

"I asked Spike to take all that stuff about you torturing cats down."

"You have a lot of nerve to say this is not your doing. It's your tweets, your posts, your website with its disgusting little cartoon image."

"Just don't look at it." He paused, then decided to tell her the truth. "Yeah. It's my doing, kind of, I guess. But I don't know if I can stop it."

She dropped her head into her hands. "You are *so* disgusting. *So* incompetent. *Such* an imbecile."

He had learned to fight back against abuse like that. "I'm going to be the vice president of America soon."

"Yeah, right. Do you think you'll be vice president when everybody finds out who Simone de Boudoir's porno sex partner, Mr. *Ramsteel,* is?" She managed this last bit of sarcasm before dropping her head right onto her keyboard. He couldn't tell if she was laughing or crying then. But she didn't look up again, and he walked away.

He wouldn't explain to Kathie what had just happened with Nell. He didn't want Kathie to start feeling guilty again for throwing Nell over and returning to her regular hetero life. More importantly, he didn't want to remind her of his new status as an influencer. It was getting harder and harder not to brag to her about his hundreds of thousands of followers, not to mention that he was soon to become vice president. But, despite her disparagement of his political career, he was starting to think she liked him.

After Mallory was seen to be hobnobbing with presidential candidate Jake De Santo, word came down from UniCast headquarters that he was not to be fired after all, Ms. Marcie told him. Harrison had taken it as a sign that he should let Mallory do as he pleased. But all this freedom had a strange effect on Mallory. He was bored. He had cut down on the Dough and Go cinnamon buns to the point that they took up only about fifteen minutes of his day, and the Cheer Committee had long ago removed anything of caloric value from the vending machines in the company break room. He certainly couldn't talk to Nell, and he had the feeling that if he hung around Kathie's cubicle too much, she might think he had nothing better to do. He decided to answer the customers' phone calls and see if he could actually help them.

"Hello, this is Kevin Mallory at UniCast Customer Assistance. How may I help you?"

It didn't go as well as he expected. In order to save UniCast the expense of sending a technician to the customer's home, he was first supposed to find out if there was some simple problem the customers could fix themselves. Every customer assistance employee, including Mallory, had a list of the parts of the customer's cable system that the customer should check. The problem was that Mallory had no idea what half of these parts were. Neither did most customers. His very first call was discouraging. He and the customer worked together for more than an hour without making any progress. He decided to eavesdrop on Nell to see if he could learn anything from her about how to do this job. But he was surprised to hear her quietly crying on the phone.

"It's Galahad," he heard her sob. "I just got back from the vet. He's got cancer."

Mallory had not-so-fond memories of dog sitting the rambunctious Irish Setter and his pug-like pal, Brute, together with Nell's three cats. He hadn't been fond of any of them except the one cat, Koko, who had since died. But he did feel sorry for Nell, who now seemed to be about to lose another of her five best friends. He got up and went to the opening of her cubicle, but she turned away, still sniffling. Upset by the whole scene, he escaped to the break room, where he spent the rest of his UniCast workday. He told himself he'd try the customer assistance thing, and Nell, again tomorrow.

Mallory was hoping that Lou would be at the dealership when he arrived there that evening. Lou was an avid supporter of Jake De Santo and American Values. He knew Mallory was connected with both, and he had instructed Rick to give him any time off he needed to further the cause. Mallory was dying to share the secret of his vice presidency with this man. But Lou wasn't there that evening.

Chapter 24: Girls' Clothing

"I was glad to hear you share our American values," was all that presidential candidate De Santo said when introduced to his vice-presidential running mate. He took Mallory's hand with all the solemnity of an undertaker meeting the bereaved. Mallory didn't like him. Anne had told him that De Santo was unhappy with having to make such an early choice for a running mate, but his numbers were slipping just as Mallory's were rising, and there was otherwise a risk that Mallory would run for president himself. She also told him not to worry about De Santo's opinion of him. There was no need for them to interact with each other at all when they weren't at rallies – and, in fact, if they won the election, there'd be no need for them to interact at all.

Their first rally, in Dubuque, Iowa, didn't go off well at all. Mallory's opening dance flourish to the tune of *Rocky* was a big hit, as was the giant video of Manic Mallory dancing and farting and swinging his braided goatee. The crowd roared "no" when he opened with: "Hey, you all like gays and LGBTs rammed down your throat?" and "Should your kid be taught there are seven sexes?" But he didn't get much of a response for his claim that teachers were making kids draw pictures of each other's genitals. Anne had warned him that people in Iowa, more than in other places, probably had a better idea of what was actually going on in their schools. She said to emphasize that the deviancy was mostly going on in other places, especially New York and California.

The crowd seemed to believe that almost anything was going on in those states. At the first mention of his website, a cry of "*Nells, Nells*" slowly grew from almost a group mumble into a shouted chant. "Save the cats!" soon followed. "Jail the *Nells*," was next. But Mallory stood mute, and the chants eventually subsided. The crowd seemed disenchanted. Mallory didn't care. He had decided he wasn't going to do the *Nell* thing anymore.

He had to rev them up with something else. "I'm here for American values. I am here for family values. I am a Martyr of God. I am here for sex between regular males and regular females!" But the crowd didn't seem too excited to hear what Mallory and the rest of God's Martyrs were *for*. He realized they wanted to be *against* something.

"Let me tell you about another travesty that we, God's Martyrs, have uncovered. Our regular, all-American children are being shamed for their normal impulses. Young boys are being punished for looking at girls' clothing – but they're being encouraged to wear it. If our children are not gay or bi, teachers look down on them." The crowd seemed to perk up. "Transvestite dances are being held on school grounds. Perversity is being foisted on our children under the guise of 'inclusion.'" A healthy chorus of boos arose from the crowd.

"Inclusion? Well, include me out! Say it with me: *Include me out!* Join God's Martyrs, join Jake De Santo in rooting out this deviance that is corrupting the America that *we* built and that *we* love so much!"

Anne told him later that "Include me out" was too complicated, and had too many syllables, for this crowd. Now, they seemed only moderately excited. The good side of that, he thought, was there seemed to be little danger that he'd be trampled. He danced around the stage again to mild applause, this time eliminating the part where he wiggled his hind parts at the crowd. The *Rocky* theme got him a modest ovation as he left.

"Let me tell you something about politics," Anne lectured him on the bus back to the airport. "You have to always be careful about what you say. Every little thing you say will be noticed by the other side, everything you do will be scrutinized, maybe even in the mainstream press."

"I have made some enemies in my time," he admitted. "But what can they do to me now? I'm the vice president."

She sighed. "Get some rest." She patted him on the shoulder and moved to another seat.

*** ***

He felt like his ship had finally come in. Spike had given him a check for $500, and American Values had paid off his last credit card. Plus, he now had two jobs. Spike was handling whatever had to be put on the internet. Anne was telling him where he had to appear next and emailing him the plane tickets. It was nice to have someone to talk to at every rally. He told her he refused to speak about *Nells* or cat torturers, and she seemed to think they could steer the crowds away from those subjects. He tried to focus his talks on the indoctrination of children into deviant sexual practices by their teachers, though he sometimes got bored with that and talked about whatever else came into his mind. He was still doing his little prancing dance on the stage at each rally, though Anne had convinced him that he shouldn't moon the audience. He was enjoying himself like never before.

But asking Kathie out on a date was still the most exciting thing he had ever done. He wanted to do it again. But she refused to talk about his political ideas or his internet fame or his vice presidency. He was used to women being disgusted with him because of his crude, animalistic behavior. But, a woman being disgusted with him for his *success*? That was an issue he had never had to face before. He decided this must be another typical female weakness.

"So, you won't go out with me anymore because you're jealous of my fame, right?" he asked her in the truck. It was the only place they talked anymore.

"I have nothing to be jealous of. You're making a fool of yourself in front of the whole country."

"So, you won't go out with me because you think I'm a fool."

"I never said I won't go out with you."

They went to Le Fromage, a restaurant downtown that cost as much as two months' meals at the Dough and Go. He wore his clean suit. She wore a green velvety dress that seemed to be daring him to slide his hands over it. Inside Fromage, he was shocked that the portions were so tiny. The waiter acted like he was an imbecile. The drinks were so microscopic he ordered several. She explained to him what some of the food was, but she didn't understand a lot of it herself, and neither of them dared ask the waiter. He had never seen Kathie so tentative before. He didn't order dessert because he knew it would be just enough to make him hungrier. He was devastated that he had spent half his cash, and all that he had accomplished was to make her unhappy.

He was hoping it was just the antagonistic ambience of the restaurant that had kept her so quiet. But she still didn't say much on the way back to his apartment. He had cleaned it up as best he could with the only cleaning tools he had, an old washcloth and a bottle of Windex. But they hadn't talked much at all in the last week, and they weren't talking now. He had known that any female would accept an offer for a free dinner at Fromage, and so he still had no idea if they were dating at all in a romantic way. He knew it was crazy to sit there in her truck wondering, instead of just asking her if she was still into him, but he was afraid.

"Why'd you ask me out again?" She said, breaking the silence.

"Um …." He didn't dare tell her again he was in love with her. There was too much to lose. His best friend. His ride to both of his jobs. He decided to answer her question with a question. If he could find out a little more about her, maybe he could figure out for himself if she might want him. "Why did you break up with Rhys?"

"I told you about me crying on the plane all the way to Mexico. Rhys and I were supposed to go together. We'd paid for the tickets and everything in advance. Then, two weeks before we were supposed to leave, he told me he lost his passport and couldn't go. We looked everywhere for it in the apartment, but we couldn't find it."

"You broke up with him just for that?"

"Let me finish." Her mouth was set in a tight line. "I still had to go. This was our family reunion. And I mean, as many problems as I had with Rhys, I had still been excited about introducing him to my brother and sister. I was sure I could find his passport somewhere. At work, we kept our relationship secret, so I searched his desk while he was out to lunch one day. I was hoping he had just misplaced it in there somewhere.

"But when I opened the middle drawer of his desk, I found his passport right there, on top of everything. There was nothing wrong with it; it was up to date. I put it right on top of his desk, where he couldn't possibly miss it. I thought he'd be so surprised."

"Was he?"

"This is the shit part. He didn't mention it that day, or that evening. I thought he was just teasing me and was going to surprise me later. I kept waiting for the surprise. But he never mentioned it. Then he drove me to the airport and just dropped me off. The real truth was, he didn't want to go on vacation together, and he lied to me about it. He never intended to go, and he didn't have the guts to tell me. I broke up with him by text from the plane. I went alone to Mexico and cried about it there with my brother and sister."

Mallory was shocked. "I can't believe he didn't want to go on a Mexican beach vacation *with you*."

"I thought I was in love with him. I tried to change for him. But I can't live with somebody who's unfaithful."

"Unfaithful? Was he screwing around with another woman while you were in Mexico?"

"I have no idea. And I don't care. No, I mean he was lying to me. Lying is being unfaithful, too."

"Oh."

The conversation stopped. He was not getting any closer to figuring out what she would want, or what he should do, when they got to his apartment. He just had to take a chance. He had to talk about what was really on his mind. "Why did you kiss me the last time we went out?"

She smiled over at him in a prelude to a laugh. "I don't know. Because you spent all that money on me at the free concert in the park?"

Mallory calculated. If she kissed him for spending nothing in the park, what would she do now for the $275 he just spent on her at Fromage? But he knew in his heart that it didn't work that way, no matter what Manly Man had taught him.

"Why don't we go back to that park again, right now?" he suggested.

"Why?"

"Um. Because I got lucky there once?"

She laughed. "You don't have to be like that. You act like it's such a weird thing that I like you. It makes me feel like there's something wrong with *me*."

"There's nothing wrong with you. You're perfect."

"No, I'm not. And that goes to show what terrible judgment you have about women, just like you have terrible judgment about *everything*. But, Kevin, what I want to tell you is, I think underneath all your crazy beliefs, you are a sweet man." No one had ever said anything like that to him before. But he didn't have time to savor that thought because she went on. "And sometimes you make me feel like maybe I'm not such a bitch."

*** ***

"You win." Nell had come in late for the second time that week. She looked like she had slept in her clothes. And her clothes looked like a long-haired Irish Setter had slept with her. Nell's customer satisfaction rating was lagging, so Mallory had convinced Kathie to temporarily boost her rating to at least average. Nell was not even aware that her customers were not happy, so there was no point in telling her any of that. "A neighbor sicced her dog on me last night," she went on. "The only place I'm safe is in this cubicle, and I hate it here. You've totally destroyed me."

"Maybe you can sue Spike. He's the one who invented the *Nell* business. I can't stop him, no matter what I say."

"Galahad is suffering. The neighbors think I'm poisoning him. My vet kicked me out of his practice. The one I'm going to now is charging me three times as much. He makes his assistant watch me in the waiting room to make sure I don't poison any of the other animals. No lawsuit is going to fix this."

"I'm sorry." This was all Mallory could think of to say. He could see that Nell was going to reject any ideas he came up with. And there was no way to convince her that he had no control over any of Spike's internet postings.

He was starting to wonder if Spike was telling him the whole truth. He was certainly lying about cutting out the *Nell* postings. And if Spike's stories of millions of followers and eager advertisers were true, it seemed he would have gotten more than a total of $800 cash out of the operation. The only people who had come through for him financially were American Values and the De Santo campaign. He wished he could talk about these things with Kathie. There was certainly no chance of talking with Nell about anything.

Chapter 25: Okay

VP candidate and media influencer Kevin Mallory already admitted jumpstarting porn star Simone de Boudoir's career. Now Simone is engaging in live sex on the internet with a character named Ramsteel. Apparently, Mallory can't tell the difference between a whorehouse and the White House.

"Bad news." It was Anne, calling him directly that night. "Senator Tung's campaign discovered Manic Mallory's internet posts recommending porn star Simone de Boudoir. And that happened just when Simone apparently switched from porn selfies to live sex on screen. So disgusting. Oh no, here's another one."

Mental Midget Mallory now a whoremaster.

Mallory was not disturbed. "I don't care. And I still recommend her. Those posts were so successful she raised her price to $99 a month. By the way, do you think American Values would pay for that subscription for me?"

Anne ignored his question. "De Santo might not want you on his ticket now."

He sought out Spike at the Dough and Go late that night. "What's the big deal? Why would De Santo drop me because of this?" he complained to his mentor. "What would single guys do if there weren't porn sites?"

"This is good news. We've had another uptick because of this story. You're almost as famous as the My Pillow guy now. And we haven't even started our counterattack."

"Maybe we should say Tung is gay? There must be some reason he doesn't like porn."

"Ha." Spike jerked his head up in surprise at Mallory's perspicacity. "That's not a bad idea."

Tung regularly shows Simone de Boudoir videos at his campaign workers' cocktail hour, but mysteriously shows no interest himself.

"I'm trying to be subtle," Spike explained. "De Santo and Tung are basically engaged in a he-man contest. Tung's *not* looking at the video *raises questions*, as the mainstream media would put it, about his masculinity."

"Uh, okay. But is Simone getting paid for these videos in the campaign room?"

"There are no porn videos in the campaign room! I made that up. Details, Kevin. Details."

Anne called again, her voice restrained like she was holding her breath at the sight of something awful on her kitchen floor. "Okay. Listen. We've convinced De Santo to see the upside of this Simone de Boudoir thing. He's going to say you have a history of helping small businesses, and that Tung is afraid of a little old Texas housewife."

"Okay."

"And your line is supposed to be that you helped her be so successful you can't afford to subscribe to her website anymore."

"But that's true."

"Yeah, but that's okay. You can still say that."

*** ***

Mallory was sick of being a candidate for vice president. He wasn't making any money from it. He had no control over the posts that Spike was creating, some of which were driving Nell into a deep depression. He recognized that his one special power, his expertise at lying his way out of any situation, was more than matched by that of De Santo and Tung. He was tired of the rallies, tired of being told what to talk about and what not to talk about. Other than the $800 Spike had given him, he had made no money from politics since American Values had paid off his old credit card debts. He wasn't enjoying his foray into politics anymore, but he knew that his own national prominence was the only thing keeping him employed at both UniCast and Lou's.

But he was happy. Kathie had come back to his apartment after their date at Fromage. He was embarrassed to offer her cognac because, between them, they both understood his long, unsuccessful history of trying to use it as a seduction potion. But it was the only thing he had to drink in his apartment.

"I'm going to taste just a little bit of that." He looked in vain for a mischievous smile when she said that. He took a little sip himself.

He felt like he was at a crossroads in his life. His tall, blonde goddess was sitting next to him on his sofa bed, but the sensations he was experiencing were not the usual. Her gorgeous breasts seemed ready to flow right out of the deep V in her green velvety dress, her neck glowed soft and kissable whenever she tossed back her curls; but something held him back from reaching for what he wanted. He wanted something else more. He didn't know what that was.

"What did you mean when you said I make you feel like you're not such a bitch? You're not a bitch."

"See? Right there. You think I'm okay."

"I don't think you're just okay. I think you're beautiful."

"I've heard that before. A lot. From guys who can't stand me in the end."

Mallory felt hollow. He hadn't realized he'd been feeding her a standard line. And he should have realized that she'd heard that a million times before. That wasn't what he really meant, anyway. "You make me feel like the regular world we're in, you know, like Lou's, and UniCast, and a free concert in the park with no-name musicians, is all okay. I know none of it is really any better than it ever was, but it's like I never noticed before that it was okay." He waited for her to lecture him, to tell him that his other world, the world of influencers and politicians and professional liars, was not okay. But she didn't.

"Tell me something." She took his hand, something that caused his heart to jump, though he tried to act casually about it. She went on. "Hasn't anybody ever told you?" she went on. "Hasn't anybody ever told you, I mean *convinced* you, that *you* are okay?"

"I'm feeling a lot better lately. I think I'm okay."

"I do, too."

"But you hate my influencer business."

She moved closer. "Can't we forget about that? Just for tonight?" She was whispering, tentative, not like the brassy Kathie he was used to. She was close enough that he could feel her breath on his neck. He turned to her. He had never been any good at guessing what a woman wanted. Now, those beautiful green eyes seemed to be pleading. Her parted lips seemed to be begging for his touch. But he knew he had never been right about this kind of thing before. He knew he had to guess exactly right this time, or most of what he cared about in the real world would be ruined.

It wasn't ruined. They started with a gentle kiss like the one they had shared in the park. He still held himself back even as she shocked him next with the deep kiss he had been fantasizing about for weeks. Then he reached a trembling hand toward that sleek blouse. She let him touch her marvelous breasts, and he even imagined he heard her moan as he stroked. His porn site had trained him to go from start to finish in seven minutes. This was the exact length of every one of Simone's postings. But Kathie was getting really excited; her hands were quivering as they helped each other strip off their clothes. When she lay before him on the bed, offering herself totally, he got so excited he had to glance away. He had to get this right, to do it right with her. He couldn't just do a seven-minute Simone. He had to do a triple Simone, or at least a double. But he couldn't keep track of how long their joy was going on. She caught him with her eyes, breathing a soft *oh oh oh* as they moved together.

Afterward, she lay with her head on his shoulder, her bombshell of curls tickling his face. He didn't move. "You know, you're different from every other man I ever met," she murmured.

"Was I pretty good?" he guessed.

"No. Not that. I mean, you're the only man in my life, including my father, who ever really talked to me."

Okay

*** ***

Lou was thrilled. "De Santo is coming to Columbia, right down the street, halfway between Baltimore and Washington. They want us to gas up and service their cars! I know they're only doing that because you work here."

"Yeah, that's right. I suggested that." He wasn't sure if he had anything to do with that at all, but Mallory didn't see any harm in letting loose his reflexive lying instinct in small matters like this.

Rick shook his head at Mallory as soon as Lou was out of sight. "You're getting away with murder, missing all these days for your campaigning. And I hear you're not getting along with the mechanics, either."

"No, that's not true."

Rick turned and walked off. "Whatever."

The dealership had finally acquired a larger wooden stand where he could rest his computer and write up tickets. As he approached, he saw that it even had a little nameplate with "Kevin Mallory" printed on it. But he failed to see the plastic bucket teetering on a shelf underneath. And the instant he laid his laptop down, the bucket fell and sloshed the glutinous contents all over his pants and shoes. The smell was so nauseating he had to run outside and lean both hands against the wall and take deep breaths to try to keep from retching. It didn't work. He pushed himself upright slowly, wiping his mouth on his shirtsleeve. His eyes were watering, and he knew he'd have to pay yet another cleaning bill for his suit. When he turned around, Victor and the young blonde mechanic he had first dealt with were in the doorway, half bent over like he had been, except they were bent over with laughter.

"Hey! How do you like our shop pet, Squirdunk?" Victor taunted him. "He's been feeling a little sick, so we thought you could take care of him."

"He's actually what's left of a racoon. He's been dead months," the young mechanic added, running fingers through his blonde hair. He was obviously the kind of person who had to explain every joke. "He was run over and mashed so bad we thought he was a squirrel at first."

Victor's grin was huge. "We added a little water. Everybody needs fluids, you know. Maybe Squirdunk can watch your station while you're off saving the world."

Mallory didn't see the humor in the situation. His anger gave him enough courage to walk right up to and between the two still-laughing mechanics. He reached the water hose and sprayed the decaying matter off his pants and shoes as best as he could, then stood back and folded his arms. He didn't say anything because he didn't have to. Victor eventually figured out that Mallory wasn't going to talk to any customers, or send any work to the mechanics, as long as that open bucket was sitting next to that stand. Mallory then watched, smirking, as Victor and the young mechanic eventually put the plastic lid on the bucket and carried it outside and around the back of the building.

He knew why they were picking on him. Kathie seemed to inspire hatred in every one of her exes. But he understood, now more than ever, how horrible it must be to enjoy the full Kathie experience and then to be cut off from her forever. The soundtrack of their lovemaking was still playing over and over in his mind. It had been a little different from what he had fantasized and, he knew now, a little different from what either of them had shared with anyone else before. He pitied Victor for losing her. He took a deep breath and powered through the day, soggy pants and all. Even if every customer he dealt with that evening seemed to be nauseated by his smell, he was happy. He was content. He was managing to deal with his new, small world. He was okay.

Chapter 26: Ramsteel Redux

Mallory now understood that Spike would keep harping on the *Nell* trope, no matter how much he objected. He wondered if therapy could do anything for Nell. He realized there was nothing he could say to help her. He remembered the point in his own therapy when Grace, that sweet young thing, accused him of thinking of women as just "animals you can fuck." He hadn't seen the problem with that attitude at first. But Grace's – and Lilly's, and Kathie's – steady friendship had eventually led him to see how much he was missing with that mindset. But now Nell seemed so depressed and bitter he doubted even the Healing Hearts could cheer her up.

Kathie was worried about Nell, too. On their drive to UniCast the next morning, she broke their embarrassed silence by asking if he'd seen Nell at work.

"How would I see her? She only comes to my cubicle when she wants to scream at me for ruining her life."

"You work right next to her. You didn't notice her own cubicle has been dark the last two days?"

"I guess she's sick or on vacation or something."

"Nell hasn't missed a day of work in eight years." Kathie pulled to a stop in the parking lot. "I think this is important. I'm going over to her house at lunchtime." She looked over at him significantly.

"What? Are you switching back again?"

She shook her head slowly like she was disappointed in him. "I knew you'd say that. You're so insecure. I want to make sure nothing has happened to her. She lives alone, you know, and her neighbors won't talk to her. She's not answering her phone." When he didn't respond, she went on, but in a much more tentative voice. "Okay, I don't just want to see her. I need to do something for her. It has to do with Galahad. I'd really like you to go over there with me and help me with it. I have to tell you, it might be really hard. I want you to bring something with you, too. I'll explain it all later, if you'll go."

He decided he'd go, even though he couldn't imagine a more awkward situation. They left at lunchtime. Even with a short detour to Mallory's apartment, the drive to Nell's house took only about fifteen minutes. She came to the door in a bathrobe, her hair looking exceptionally ragged without the discipline of those barrettes. The house was a mess. They followed her into the kitchen area. Her two remaining cats, Florence and Kiki, who usually reacted to visitors by racing around the room pretending to be afraid of Galahad, Nell's Irish Setter, were quietly making themselves look small on the sofa. But their eyes were big, as if hoping their visitors would solve the problem in the room. Galahad was lying on the area rug in front of the sofa, emanating a foul smell, his breathing rapid. Brute, the squat little mutt who usually spent all his indoor time barking at any noises outside, was nonchalantly resting in the corner.

Nell looked like she didn't know what to say to these two people, her ex-lover and her ex-suitor, who had shown up at her door so unexpectedly together. Mallory and Kathie exchanged glances. They hadn't talked about who would speak first, or what tack they would take if things were as bad as they now looked.

"Please go away." Nell didn't look either of them in the eye.

Kathie had the nerve to speak first. "We were just worried about you."

"And Galahad," Mallory added. "We know he's in pain."

"*I'm* in pain. Thanks to you, Mallory, all the kids in the neighborhood think I'm poisoning Galahad. They've called the police on me twice." She tightened the sash on her robe, stared at the floor. Kathie approached her very slowly and put her arms out to caress her, but Nell backed away. "You think that's going to make me feel good, Kathie? After you said you loved me? And you were just faking it. To humiliate me. Well, it worked. I have nothing in my life now but my dogs and cats, and Galahad's dying, and Brute doesn't seem to care."

Nell sobbed, then suddenly turned around and laid her head

on the counter, face down. Kathie looked at Mallory like it was his turn to try. He carefully moved next to her. He had once dreamed of holding her in his arms, but he was now terrified of even touching her. He looked back at Kathie. She gently shrugged as if she had no idea what to do. Galahad's raspy breathing was the only sound in the house. He wanted to say that at least *he* had loved her, but that didn't mean anything to anybody now. He tried to think of something, anything to help. She picked up her head from the counter when he came close.

"You can't let Galahad go on suffering like this," he began.

"Don't you understand? Nobody will take him! No vet will even let me in his office now! The minute he got sick, the neighbors called the police for suspected animal cruelty. They think I'm poisoning him – just like you're saying online."

Mallory glanced over at Kathie, but she shook her head. There was no point in defending himself here and now. No matter what he was guilty of, the issue right then was Galahad.

"We feel sorry for Galahad, too. That's why we came here. Kathie and I will take him. Kathie's uncle has a 70-acre farm in western Maryland. He's agreed to euthanize him and give him a decent burial. For free."

"How would he do it?" He could hear a small catch of relief in her voice.

"Quickly. With my rifle. I have it in the truck."

Nell's head sunk lower again until she was staring down at the floor. Her voice was tiny. "If that happens, I want to be there."

Mallory had a quick, desperate hope that Kathie and Nell would do this grisly business together and leave him out of it.

"But," Nell added, "I don't want either of you around." Mallory was glad to hear that, but Kathie looked like she had been struck another blow. Nobody seemed to know what to do. Nell raised her head and took a long, deep breath, not looking at either of them. "I can't watch him suffering any longer. I'll take him there myself. I don't want either of you to be there."

"So, how ...?"

"Call your uncle," she commanded Kathie.

Kathie arranged for her uncle to meet Nell and Galahad at the bottom of his driveway in an hour and a half. Nell refused to take Kathie's truck. She insisted she would drive herself so Galahad would take his last ride in the comfort of her car. But Mallory's mouth dropped open when Nell then asked him to carry Galahad to the back seat of her car. He gagged at the thought and reflexively turned away. He had assumed Kathie would do the honors with the actual moving of the sick dog.

He was afraid he wasn't strong enough to lift the Irish Setter in one piece, afraid he'd make his pain worse, afraid that poor Galahad would snap at him. But Nell had him sit on the sofa while she gradually pulled the dog, shoulders first, then hindquarters, onto his lap. Galahad then looked up, questioning him with big, rheumy eyes. Mallory hadn't seen such a sorrowful look in his whole life. He didn't know how to react. But he took a deep breath and used the power of his pity to force himself to a standing position with Galahad in his arms. Then he staggered, with a woman on each side helping support him, out to Nell's car.

They placed him so that Nell could see him from the driver's seat on his last ride. He didn't even resist when they buckled seatbelts clumsily around his body. Kathie asked Nell if she was sure she wanted to do this alone. Nell's "yes" was only a little less antagonistic than before. Mallory remembered how Galahad's goofy rambunctiousness had made dog sitting for Nell such an adventure. He felt that all the animosity between the three humans seemed petty compared to the suffering of this creature.

They put the rifle in the trunk of her car, and she drove off without a word.

*** ***

V.P. candidate and influencer Kevin Mallory has been outed as the real "Ramsteel," the onscreen sex partner of porn star Simone de Boudoir.

"Don't worry. They have a video, but it's clearly consensual," Anne assured him. "Tung sent that tweet, but he doesn't know what to do with the story. And both candidates have long histories of sleazy relationships. Their constituents aren't offended at all." When Mallory didn't respond, she went on, a little more tentatively. "By the way, was that really you on the video? I couldn't really tell because of the mask."

Mallory was impressed that she cared. "Yeah, I'm Ramsteel." He hoped there wouldn't be any mention of toadstools.

"Someone must have leaked that it was you."

He loved her for a second then for being so non-judgmental. "I know who leaked it. An ex-friend of mine at work. She's hated me for months now."

"As I said, the candidates don't really care, but American Values might. I mean, not really, but they don't want to seem to be condoning having sex with prostitutes."

"She's not a prostitute. What do you want me to do?"

"Just keep quiet about the whole thing."

But De Santo didn't. He immediately tweeted.

Our Macho Mallory has made a poor Texas housewife rich!

De Santo was defending Mallory, just as Anne had predicted. Mallory got a little bump in his number of followers. He begged Spike to follow Anne's advice and ignore the story.

"Are you kidding? You've been telling the country about its enemies for weeks. Now it's time to show people what's right, what's good about this country, your true colors, what a real heterosexual man you are."

"I do think I looked rather manly. The camerawork was much better than …." He decided not to tell Spike about his homemade selfie video that Kathie had seen.

"*Of course* you looked manly."

Senator Tung should shut his mouth and study the video to see how a real man satisfies a real woman. Or is he not interested in that?

Mallory didn't usually look at anything Spike posted, but he looked at this one and liked it – after he figured out that he was being called a real man.

Anne told him that his poll numbers were up slightly since the Simone incident had surfaced. Because of that, American Values was not going to push to get him off the ticket. "The *Macho Mallory* thing is working for you. American Values is basically afraid to say anything against you, and they're still 100% behind De Santo. So, we're still good to go."

He noticed the sour turn of her lips when she said that. He knew Anne was probably as disgusted with his cavorting with Simone as Kathie would be. But she wouldn't tell him that. Her job was to keep the American Values candidates on track to win the primary. To keep him on track, she had to pretend that he was a manly role model – or at least a normal American male. But he wondered if he made it even into that normal category in her mind. She was too smart to be influenced by his Macho Mallory foolishness, but she still seemed to like him. For a long time now, he had been living in two completely different worlds. He had been entertaining fantasies of having a different woman in each. But the world that Spike had pushed him into, he now decided, was too ugly. He didn't even want a woman who was in that world anymore. Not even the spectacular Anne. Giving up on that idea eased the tension between him and Anne so much he found it downright pleasant to talk with her.

"Actually," he confessed to her now, "I'd like to get out of this politics business."

Anne looked to the side, took a deep breath. When she turned back, she had a tiny smile on her face like she was trusting him with something she had been holding back. "Actually, I'd like to quit, too. At least this particular campaign." Her steady gaze caught the surprise in his eyes. He broke into a big smile.

"So, why don't we both quit?"

"I love politics. I love campaigning. But I do not love American Values. Or De Santo, or Tung. Or Macho Mallory, to tell the truth. But this is my first big job. If I walk away from it, I'll be branded as a quitter. And a quitter will never be picked up by a major campaign again."

Mallory was quite familiar with hating one's job. He had always reacted by doing as little work as possible. But Anne obviously didn't believe in that theory. Her career was like a ladder she wanted to climb, and she wasn't going to jump off just because the first rung was covered in shit. This was a new theory to him, and he thought he might want to see how it worked out.

"Okay, I'll stick with it as long as you will," he told her then.

Chapter 27: Fluids for DeSanto

Mallory had never heard of Sean Forester before, but he was apparently one of UniCast's top managers. He had flown in from Texas to speak to the local employees, about fifty of whom were assembled in the break room, while the rest were encouraged to watch on Zoom. An uneasy feeling permeated the entire building as the tall man in the grey suit and grim smile stood before them. Mallory had just learned that Harrison had resigned the day before, leaving his subordinates with the blatantly fictitious message that he had enjoyed the challenges of working at UniCast and would treasure his many fond memories of the dedicated employees who had made being their manager such a pleasure.

Mallory heard the loud complaining as soon as he got to the door of the break room. People were already trying to shout down Forester, who stood, stone-faced, reiterating that the Maryland branch would be closed but that laid off employees would have a chance to bid on new openings in the San Diego and Spokane offices. Rhys Davies, the building manager, shouted a question above the crowd noise. Would there be positions in those offices for mid-level managers like himself? Forester quieted the crowd by answering. Frankly, he doubted it.

"What about the statistical unit?" Mallory shouted from the arched entryway to the break room. He was thinking about Kathie. Kathie was sitting near the back of the room, already looking depressed.

"We are laying off statistical people throughout the company." Forester seemed to be trying to answer in a flat voice, but there was a slight tremor of anxiety. "We've found there is a lot of duplicative effort in that area, nationwide. And we believe that artificial intelligence can handle a substantial part of that type of work from now on."

"Who is this *we*?" Mallory shouted angrily. "You're not losing your own job, are you? I bet you've been promised a big raise if the takeover by Everdine goes through." Mallory had gained some skill in guessing the mood of a crowd and bringing its rage to a boil. Shouts of "you scum" and "rich bastard" rang out.

Forester admitted that he would profit if the takeover was completed. He stood, obviously a little shaken, as the crowd grumbled on. But he gathered himself together and went on. "I didn't have to come here. I could have just notified the whole branch by email that it was being shut down. But coming here has been a sobering thing. I think I'm learning as much here today about the business as you are."

Kathie stood up and walked right past Mallory and out of the room, tears in her eyes. Before he could react, he saw Rhys turn and follow her. Mallory joined the long, slow-speed chase that turned out to be headed toward the women's room. The three of them found themselves alone in a corridor at the back of the building. Rhys raced ahead of Kathie and stood, blocking her way, his pale skin quickly reddening, his breath coming fast.

"What do you want?" she asked her tormentor. The tremor in her voice kicked up in Mallory a rage like none he had ever felt before.

"I wasn't good enough for you." Rhys's tone was ugly. "Now I want to see the look on your face now that they've put you down, too."

Mallory could see from behind her that her shoulders were shaking. He was shaking too, because he knew what he had to do. He stepped between the two of them, into the space that was barely wide enough for a man of his girth. He moved forward until he was six inches away from the taller man. His eyes were level with Rhys's beard – which, he noted with some satisfaction, was starting to turn grey. He forced himself to meet his eyes. "Let her alone!" His voice didn't come out nearly as commanding as he had hoped.

Rhys snickered. "I could wipe the floor with your ass."

Mallory was certain that was true. But Kathie was standing right behind him. He didn't have any choice in the matter. He stood there, shaking, ready to be beaten.

Rhys was still breathing heavily, but the stare-down lasted less than half a minute. "You're not worth beating up, you pathetic man. You can have that controlling bitch." He turned to walk away, but then turned back. "And good luck supporting your unemployed whore."

*** ***

Ms. Marcie found Kathie and Mallory still holding each other in the empty back corridor. She approached them like somebody who had no choice. They turned and faced her, posed casually with their arms around each other's waist as if they did this every day.

"I just wanted to tell you, Mr. Mallory," she began, speaking in such a timid voice they had to move closer to hear. "I don't want to be presumptuous, but I think you might not be familiar with all the workings of this office. And I want you to know that I'm here to help you familiarize yourself with all your new duties."

"What new duties? What are you talking about?"

"Your new duties as Acting Supervisor of Customer Service."

"What!"

"Mr. Harrison recommended you as he left. Don't worry. They're closing down this whole branch in sixty days anyway. I can help you keep things going until then."

*** ***

"Interesting news. There's going to be a De Santo rally in Columbia, halfway between Baltimore and Washington." Anne sat down with him after their most recent rally. "It'll be close enough to D.C. to get the national press but, with your local connections, close enough to get the Baltimore press, too."

"Oh. Good. I guess."

"Can I talk to you about something personal?"

Mallory's ears pricked up. "Of course." She was the only person he enjoyed talking with on the campaign trail.

"The things you're saying about teachers, that they're having choose-your-sex parties, and all that stuff. I found out. Those things just aren't true. My mother's a teacher. She said that's a complete lie. She told me to stop it."

"Your mother? But don't you read *God's Truth*?"

"No. And let me tell you something else. Nobody in this campaign reads *God's Truth* either, except to look for shit to say that's more outrageous than what the last guy said."

"Spike told me the outrageous stuff is what got me popular in the first place."

"Yeah. People love that stuff. And you're a great entertainer. But it's all made-up stuff. Lies, in other words."

"Lies." Mallory tossed that word around in his mind. How could the secret to his success be all lies? But he trusted Anne more than anyone in his political life. Now she was telling him that *God's Truth* wasn't the real truth. But *God's Truth* was working for him. He couldn't just throw it all over. "Tell me one thing on *God's Truth* that you know for sure is a lie," he challenged her.

"Okay. Let me tell you this." She gritted her teeth in an expression he had never seen on her before. "My mother, who I haven't talked to in weeks, called me last night. She was crying."

"What do you mean? Crying about what?"

"About the teachers. My mother's a teacher. She said she's not forcing children to choose what sex they are or making them watch transvestite performances. She's not telling them their genitals are as malleable as Play Doh. None of that stuff you're talking about is happening in the schools, she told me. And, you know, she's been teaching for twenty years. She's never even heard of any teacher doing things like that. And it's upsetting her. She said she was disappointed in me." Anne's own voice broke on those last words. She looked like she was about to cry herself. She swallowed hard. "Please. Lay off the teachers. For my mother. And as a favor to me, Kevin. Please."

Anne was the only person in his internet-political life whom he trusted. If she said teachers weren't forcing children to watch transvestite performances, then it wasn't happening.

*** ***

After he stared down Rhys in the corridor at UniCast after the meeting about the closure of their office, Kathie had thrown herself into his arms, sobbing. "They've been telling me for years that I'm so good at my job, but now, nobody needs me anymore."

"*I* need you."

She took him right back to her apartment then, and into her bedroom, where she made him prove it. That was the easiest assignment he had ever had. He loved that she was so bossy everywhere else but so eager to please him in bed. She seemed to be open to anything, and her eagerness inflamed his passion, and his passion fired her desire even more. They were both soon lying quietly in each other's arms, wrung out, breathless, mute. Later, in a moment of supreme contentment, he admitted to her that he wasn't happy to go back to his political world again, but he had no choice but to keep up his internet and political games, which were fueling each other. "Now more than ever, now that we both are losing our jobs at UniCast, we need the money."

"But it's all such bullshit," she shot back. "How can you stand it? And why do you keep doing this cat brutality thing? The *Nell* thing."

"Spike's the one who's doing it, not me. I've told him to stop a million times."

"Kevin, you saw her. She's really hurting. My uncle said she was a total wreck when she brought Galahad up to his farm. She couldn't watch when he did it, and when she tried to go back for one last look, she almost collapsed. He had to catch her. He was worried she wouldn't make it home. And listen. Spike's posts are getting worse. Now he's saying all the *Nells* have signed a witches' covenant to mutilate all the cats they can catch."

When Mallory confronted him at their Saturday night meeting, Spike admitted as much. "Yeah, I said that. So what? It worked. We were starting to sag, but the thing about witches dismembering cats bumped us right back up. That's how the internet world works, Kevin. If we don't have outrage, we don't have a brand anymore."

Mallory was shocked that you could make real money doing something so purely evil. He couldn't talk this over with Kathie. He knew she didn't quite believe that Spike was totally out of his control. One thing he liked about Anne was she seemed to understand that he was just a sort of a pawn being pushed around by Spike and De Santo and American Values. She didn't mock him for it, and in fact she seemed to feel like she was a sort of pawn herself. He dreaded the rally coming up, but at least Anne would be there to commiserate with him.

Lou was excited about servicing the limousines for the whole De Santo entourage at his dealership. He showed De Santo's advance man around the premises like the man was a celebrity himself. Lou promised he'd give the campaign free oil changes. Half of the mechanics' bays were closed off to accommodate the four giant Suburbans, and he ordered all of them to be washed, then kept inside so they wouldn't get dirty before the day of the rally.

"Should we change all the fluids on those limos, too?" Mallory asked Rick. He immediately realized he shouldn't have said anything. "*Your* limos," his manager grumbled. "They're taking up half of our mechanics' bays. There goes half our business, half our commissions for three days. All to keep *your* limos from getting dusty."

"They aren't my limos," Mallory protested, but Rick had already walked on. The mechanics were also blaming him for the interruption of their income stream. Victor sauntered up to him and asked him sarcastically which one was his. "I don't know," Mallory said truthfully. "But they put placards on the dashboard to show whose limo is whose."

"Oh yeah? One of these limos is yours, right? You gonna reimburse us for our lost commissions for your personal limo sitting here all week?"

"Um, no. I don't have any money."

Mallory was told to write up the regular customers' estimates but to be vague about when their cars would be finished. Rick told him that every customer, man or woman, lawyer or non-lawyer, needed all possible fluids that week. The customers' cars were still taken in and parked somewhere, stockpiling commissions for the mechanics for when the big political event was over. But then the lot boys were angry at having to constantly shuffle around so many cars on the crowded outside lot.

Mallory was probably the only one excited by having the limousines in the shop. Late that evening, after most of the other workers had gone home, he decided to take a look at these Suburban RVs that the campaign was providing. He took the key fobs to all four of them from the wall near the parts desk and started exploring them one by one. Each car had a placard on the dash indicating who that car was for. At first, Mallory couldn't see any difference between the cars. They were all huge, black limousines with three rows of seats. But then he noticed there was a fairly large wicker basket sitting on the second row of seats in the limo marked as De Santo's. Curious, he pressed the button to pop the hatch door. There he saw what was to go in the basket: a bag of Cheetos, a whole case of peanut M&Ms, a huge package of red licorice, a small box of Jolly Ranchers, and tiny bottles of bourbon, rye, Scotch – and cognac! Mallory held back his excitement until he could look over what else was in there. But the only other interesting thing he saw was an oblong, silvery bucket with rounded edges, inscribed with the word "champagne" in an overdone flowery script.

Mallory was rushing back to his own limo to see if the campaign had provided him the same kind of free treats when the customer phone rang on his stand. He raced across the floor to answer it. The customer wanted to know if his car was done.

"Yeah, it's done. But it's parked out on the lot somewhere. I don't know exactly where. Maybe you can call back tomorrow."

"I need the car tonight. I'm coming in." The customer hung up. Mallory spent the next half hour searching the scores of cars in Lou's overcrowded lot for the customer's car. By the time he found it and settled with the customer, it was almost closing time. He didn't have time to do any more exploration of the limousines, but he figured out a way to make sure that he got his share of the free goodies. All he had to do was switch the placards.

Chapter 28: Vigilantes

News Flash! Mallory disguised himself as "Ramsteel" to engage in public sex with prostitute Simone de Boudoir. This is the cowardly degenerate that De Santo has chosen for V.P.

"We will ignore that one," Spike instructed. "That's Tung, just trying again. He can't come up with anything new. That really shows how weak he is."

"I don't like being called a coward."

"Hey, you give flak, you gotta be ready to take flak."

Mallory guessed Spike was right about that, so he relaxed. He felt even more relaxed when he realized that Spike, who had watched from twenty feet away his whole encounter with Simone, hadn't noticed it was fake. Spike went on dispassionately. "They're running out of ways to attack you. But they're still trying hard. And I gotta warn you. There's been some chatter about Tung supporters disguising themselves as De Santo men and coming to the next rally to harass you."

"They'd be fools to do that. All those hefty women at the rallies love me. They'd beat the hell out of anybody who attacked me."

Mallory was more worried about what he had to say next. He knew he had to confront Spike. Nell had made it into work only three days in the last week. She obviously hadn't been washing her hair. She put her hands over her ears when he tried to tell her he was sorry about Galahad. Without a word, she had reached into her pocketbook and pulled out her phone and showed him Spike's latest post.

ALERT! ALERT! ALERT!

The Nells, that well-known nationwide coven of witches, are practicing surgical procedures to modify the sex organs of cats to satisfy their own foul cravings. They are calling for thousands of cats for these experiments, which will be carried out in dark basements under unsanitary conditions and with crude cutting tools. This may well be going on in your neighborhood. It's time to fight back. The solution is simple.

The police will do nothing to stop this. It is up to us cat owners to join together and stop this brutality ourselves! Form your C-Teams now! March on every Nell's house. Save our cats!

"My neighbors are following your posts, Kevin," she said. They haven't gone on my property yet, but they're walking back and forth on the sidewalk in front of my house."

"Can't they legally do that?"

"Yeah. That's what the police say. They do it even at night. They shine flashlights all over my house, and even in my windows. When I got out of the car yesterday a man came up to me. He said he was a member of C-Team and asked how many cats I was torturing in the basement." Her anger soon turned to tears. "Florence and Kiki are terrified, and Brute never stops barking."

"And we're all losing our jobs." Mallory added. In the midst of his politico-internet fantasy life, he hadn't really thought about how bleak things had gotten in his real life. And in Nell's real life. And in Kathie's.

Spike had told him that outrage was his brand, and he knew that the cat people's outrage was the source of most of his money – or to be more accurate, Spike's company's money. He still hadn't passed the $850 threshold yet as far as his own finances were concerned. He left work immediately after his conversation with Nell and headed for the Dough and Go.

"Take it down!" he screamed at Spike. "I'm ordering you to take it down now. The neighbors are torturing Nell. Her cats are having nervous breakdowns."

"No can do." Spike's voice was flat.

"It's my website."

"Not exactly." Mallory could hear the sneer in Spike's voice. "I own the internet domain that we use. I also own the trademarks on Mad Mallory and Manic Mallory and Macho Mallory. And on *Nell*. All the money coming in from the Cat-A-Tonic people is legally mine. And the money is pouring in. Why would I stop it?"

"Because it's driving the cat lovers in this country crazy. They're talking about forming feline protection militias. It's just dangerous."

"Details! Didn't I tell you not to bother about the details? The cat people love the *Nell* thing. They want a reason why their precious cats get sick, why they die, why they disappear. They need somebody to blame. We're giving them somebody to blame. We're giving them what they need, and they're paying us for it."

"You're going to go on doing this forever." Mallory was certain of this now. He felt defeated.

"I know how to stir people up. It's something I'm good at. I'm thinking about school cafeteria ladies next. Everybody hates their lunches. Maybe I'll claim they're doing stuff to the kale."

*** ***

As soon as he arrived for the rally, Anne came up to him with startling news. "Something has happened to De Santo. He's throwing up out back. You're going to have to go on first and keep talking until he can make it to the stage."

"What happened?"

"They don't know, exactly. Everybody who was in the limousine is sick. They think it might have something to do with the cats."

"What cats?"

"There's a weird group of people concerned about cats. You'll see them. They all have *C-Team* on the front of their t-shirts."

"Oh. I know about the C-Team. But why are there actual cats here?"

"They come from the Howard County animal shelter. The C-Team wanted them here. They want people to adopt them, at the rally. De Santo said to let them do it."

"So, you think the cats made everybody in the limo sick?"

Anne shrugged.

"How long do I have to talk to this crowd until De Santo comes on?"

"Nobody knows. He's still barfing."

Chapter 29: Cataclysm

Mallory decided the situation called for prolonged prancing around the stage. He raised his fist repeatedly as the *Rocky* theme played. Pointing to the Macho Mallory character on the screen behind him, he tried to jump in sync with the character's every move, all to the delight of the crowd – until the second time he went through the entire *Rocky* song. Then the cheers died down. He knew he'd have to say something.

"Um, we have some cats here. The good people at the C-Team here," he paused and gestured toward the crowd of about twenty team members. "They borrowed them from the local animal shelter here. Anybody who wants to adopt a cat, come right up to the side of the stage here and pick one out." There was no reaction but silence. Mallory figured he had done his duty toward the cats.

"Have you ever wondered," he began, "what the *plus* is in LGBTQ-plus? It's an invention, folks." He was parroting what he'd read on *God's Truth* the night before. "I'll tell you why it was invented. The people who made up the *plus* needed to make room for any kind of perversion they hadn't thought of yet. So, I guess they want to lump into the category of *plusses* people who fornicate with cats, child molesters, mother rapists, people who believe God is coming down from the clouds and messing with their privates. We used to burn these people at the stake in the name of God. Then we just made it illegal. Then we said it was legal, but just told them to keep quiet about it. Now, by God, they have *parades. Government-sponsored* parades!" He stomped his foot to make sure he got a big crowd reaction.

"The government and the media are teaching our kids to worship these perversions! The government in California has banned the terms 'man' and 'woman' and 'boy' and 'girl' from all public discussion. I guess everyone's a 'unit' now. And we're told that the units can clump together for sex in any way they want, in any numbers, like a bunch of single-cell bacteria. But I say, enough is enough!" He hoped the crowd didn't notice that he'd left out any mention of teachers, at Anne's request.

"Want to hear something?" He pretended to look at his phone. "Want me to read to you the first words of the new bible required by the State of California?"

And God created Unit 1, but Unit 1 was lonely, and so God created Unit 2 to interact with Unit 1; but Unit 1 was empowered to change itself into a Unit 2, and Unit 2 was empowered to change into a Unit 1.

And God looked down on these degenerate creatures and said, "Hey, whatever."

He did get a short laugh, but he had run out of things to say. He looked at Anne for inspiration. He was searching for more words to stir up the indignation of the crowd. But he realized what his real problem was. He didn't feel indignant anymore. He felt fortunate.

With a little luck, and a lot of help from Spike, he had brought in more money recently than almost any other influencer – and certainly way more than the mainstream editors and reporters whom he was always accusing of lying. He had made a new friend in Anne, a woman so smart and canny she saw through all the bullshit her clients were trying to spread around the country. He was beginning to learn the ropes at UniCast and Lou's, something he had never managed to do at his thirteen previous jobs. And, most of all, he had Kathie.

Anne now shrugged in response to his glance, signaling she also didn't have any ideas about how to keep the speech going. She pointed back to the staging area and mimed someone throwing up. Apparently, De Santo was not quickly recovering from his sudden illness. Mallory glanced down at the C-Team members, most of whom were crowded up near the stage. He hated them. He knew he was partially responsible for Nell's problems. But they were the ones who were actually torturing Nell. He ordered the Manic Mallory cartoon and the music to be stopped.

"So, let's get this cat adoption started!" he yelled into the mike. He ran over to Anne and demanded she talk to the Animal Control people. She rolled her eyes at first; but after he challenged her to come up with a better idea, she did as he asked. Soon, the entire abandoned cat population of Columbia was brought out in cages onto the stage.

"Who wants to save one of these cute little tabbies?" When no one responded, he pointed directly at the group nearest the stage. "C'mon, C-Team. Don't tell me not one of you cat vigilantes wants to save a single little cat?" He swung his arm in an arc to indicate the whole crowd. "Does no one at all here want to rescue a little tabby?"

He dragged one cage to the front of the stage and sat down, dangling his legs over the edge. He ignored the security officer warning him not to do that. He pulled a beautiful calico cat out of its cage and held it to his chest, stroking it gently. The cat seemed to like him, and he entertained a passing thought of keeping it for himself. But he knew he had to keep the show going. "Nobody wants this beautiful creature?"

Now that he was closer to them, he noticed that the C-Team was almost all men. They looked more like aging members of a street gang than a cat lovers club. But there was one member standing front and center, a frail-looking woman with grey hair who really did look like a little old cat lady. He thought he'd focus on her and pull out all the stops. He ordered all the cages brought out to the edge of the stage.

"See all these beautiful cats? Well, Animal Control has informed me that any cats not adopted by the end this rally will be euthanized tonight. If you don't want a pile of dead cats on your conscience, come on up and pick one right now!"

"Oh no!" The old woman looked appropriately alarmed. "Oh, no." He asked her to come forward, but she stopped a few steps short of the stage. "C'mon, Miss. Tabby loves you. I can tell." Mallory held the cat out to her. She took it and held it tentatively in her arms at first, but after she got a good look at the beautiful creature she was holding, she couldn't hold back a warm smile. She pulled it to her chest and embraced it like she had given birth to it. "Thank, you, Ma'am." Mallory's eyes scanned the crowd as he voiced his response as loud as he could. "Thank you, Ma'am, for saving this beautiful cat.

"Who's next? Who else wants a new smile on their face and a new friend in their home tonight? Who knows, maybe in their bed." He threw a second cat into the arms of a burly C-Team member who stood next to the old woman. "They're all dead tonight if you don't save them!" The burly man seemed stunned, but he held onto the flying feline.

Mallory thought it was fantastic that people could catch cats like that.

"They'll all be drowned in the lake by nine tonight if you don't take one now. C'mon, let's go. Let's see how much the C-Team really loves cats!"

Mallory threw another cat. This time, the target C-Team member shrank back, but he was obviously trying not to throw the cat to the ground in front of everybody. Instead, he tried to sort of juggle it. The cat sensed it was losing its balance and frantically dug its claws into the man's chest. The man roared in pain and the cat dropped down, landed on its feet and ran away, causing a visible ripple of panic to string through the crowd from front to back.

He picked up another cat even as some of the C-Team members seemed to be backing away. "If you C-Team people love your fucking cats so much, why don't you take one of these poor pussies home?" He threw the cat at the closest C-Team member. This guy didn't even pretend to want the cat, but the cat landed, claws first, and got a good grip on the man's chest before he pulled it off. The other C-Team members started quickly moving back, crowding against the De Santo people behind them.

Mallory held out another cat, a skinny, tawny, mangy thing that looked like it wouldn't live past nine o'clock whether it was thrown into the lake or not. "One more little kitty. Take it, you bunch of cowards!" But the C-Team had backed away too far for him to safely toss it. He figured this part of the show was over. Then one more team member stepped forward and reached out with muscular, tattooed arms. When Mallory leaned forward to hand him his new pet, however, the man batted the animal down. When Mallory looked up in surprise, the man grabbed Mallory's collar and pulled him roughly off the stage.

He saw a flash of light as his head and shoulder hit the concrete hard. He heard the security guard yell something. He knew he had to get up. He got his arms and legs under himself for a second, but then another man who was being pushed by the C-Team tripped and fell over him. The two of them lay entangled on the ground, facing a forest of oncoming bodies. The frightened cat wriggled its way out of his arms and shot away through a gap in the looming legs. The security guard was yelling in vain for people to stop pushing. Mallory had a frightening flashback to his first rally. Once again, a gang of overwrought political nutcases seemed ready to trample him.

Ignoring the pain in his shoulder, Mallory forced himself onto his hands and knees again. With his good arm, he grabbed the belt of the security guard and pulled himself up. Together, they pulled up the other fallen man. All three were pressed against the stage. Mallory could see a whole contingent of security guards trying to edge their way toward them. Another security guard was on the stage, hollering something. Mallory realized he was trying to talk to him.

"You're bleeding, sir. Let me help pull you up here. You might need an ambulance." The man reached out his arms but didn't have the strength pull him back up onto the stage. Mallory wished he had lost more weight. But the crush was too tight anyway. The phalanx of security guards finally managed to push the mass of bodies back. The other fallen man was shaken and out of breath, but he didn't seem to be seriously hurt.

"Thank you," the man shouted at the security guard. Then he turned and shouted to Mallory also. "Thank you, too. You're a good man."

The security contingent offered to escort Mallory back to the stage, or take him to the hospital, whichever he wished. Mallory said he just wanted to gather himself before he went anywhere. They left one guard with him. The C-Team had pretty much fled the scene by then. The guard insisted on looking closely at Mallory's wounds. Mallory put his hand to his head and felt blood; but, after walking his fingers slowly and painfully through Mallory's hair, the guard told him the bleeding had stopped.

"You should still get yourself checked out, sir."

"No. I'm okay. I just want to get out of this place."

"I can call you an ambulance, sir."

"No. If you can just do one thing for me." Mallory asked him to take him as quickly as possible to the nearest exit.

"Are you sure you're safe to drive, sir?"

"Sure. Just let me get out of here. Get some air."

Reluctantly, the guard pulled Mallory by one hand through the now-disorganized crowd toward the exit. Fortunately, neither of them was a tall man, and so very few in the crowd had a good enough view to recognize them.

"Thank you, man. We – me and that other guy – could have got really hurt if you hadn't stopped it."

"Drive safely, sir."

"Righto." But Mallory wasn't driving, and he couldn't see any of the limos. He needed to get out of sight so desperately he decided to walk.

Chapter 30: Race for the Exit

There was a half-mile asphalt driveway that snaked through the tall trees from the rally venue to the road. Mallory's face and shoulder still hurt, but he told himself his legs were fine. He wasn't more than halfway back to the road when two cars stopped for him. One pulled up in front and the other from behind.

"I got this." Anne, from the car behind him, got out of her car first and called to the woman in the car in front, who was Kathie. "I'm with the De Santo campaign. We can get him medical help, or whatever he needs."

"I'm Kathie, his girlfriend."

They walked toward each other until they met at the object of their attention. "I'm okay, really," he said. "I guess I could use a ride." He had trouble focusing on the situation because Kathie's word, "girlfriend," was echoing in his mind.

"Who should …?" The women both spoke at the same time, then stopped and looked at each other. Mallory sensed a slight tension in the air, like they didn't want to look like they were fighting over him.

"We have to hurry. The campaign staff and the press will be all over us." Anne looked back up the driveway like she expected to see them any second. "I know a place they'll never look. Kevin, go with your girlfriend. You two follow me."

Mallory's state of shock was not due to anything that happened at the rally. Kathie had said she was his girlfriend! He hadn't even dreamed she felt this way. Of course, they had been together in bed, but he knew from his experience how little that sometimes meant. Yet now, she wasn't acting any differently. She seemed to be concentrating on following Anne's car. They wound through suburban roads and through housing developments until they came to a small strip mall. They parked in front of a place called Raleigh's Bookstore and Café. "We're safe here," Anne explained. "None of those people would ever set foot in a bookstore."

They sat down inside, and Anne insisted on buying everybody coffee. She asked Mallory if she should go to the drugstore next door and buy him something for the scrapes on his face, but he said he'd rather have a doughnut. Kathie just shook her head. Anne gave her a curious glance. They all sat silently awaiting their coffee.

Anne finally broke the silence. "Kevin, I really appreciate that you didn't go on your usual *teachers-are-corrupting-students* rant this time."

"I can't believe you said that, Anne. You're actually trying to find something nice to say about what just went on? You are a real diplomat." Kathie shook her head.

Anne dropped her politic voice. "That had to be the worst fiasco of a rally in the history of campaigns." She started chuckling, then laughing, then couldn't stop. "After you left, somebody yelled 'free the cats,' and people tried to rush the stage. They were pushing and shoving with the security guards. The cats were screeching, and the Animal Control people were stumbling all over each other on the stage, trying to get the cats away from that crowd."

"That's my last rally," Mallory announced. "You can tell De Santo I quit." Both women looked over at him. "No. I mean it. I quit. And, Anne, you should quit, too. Politics is shit. You know that better than I do."

"Politics is important. I can't quit it."

"But why do you work for such a demagogue?" Kathie asked.

"You think De Santos is a demigod?" Mallory interrupted.

"No. No." The women explained to him what a demagogue was.

"Oh." This new thought caused Mallory to drop out of the conversation.

Anne sighed. "To answer your question, Kathie …. They say you have to start somewhere. American Values pays me well, and I've learned so much about campaigns."

"But we have a *friend*," Kathie quickly glanced at Mallory when she used that word. "We have a friend. Her name is Nell. The campaign is claiming she kidnaps and does experiments on cats. That group you saw at the rally, the C-Team, they're harassing her, day and night. They've made her life miserable."

"That's not the campaign doing that." Anne's tone was defensive.

"The campaign is feeding off all that outrage, and you know it."

Stares all around. Anne took a long sip of her coffee, examined her fingernails, tapped the table. "You're right," she said, meeting first Kathie's eyes, then Mallory's. "This whole thing is causing real damage. I guess I have to figure out what that means for me. As far as my career goes."

Mallory wanted another doughnut. Anne went out to the parking lot to make some calls and "to think."

"I'm surprised you came to the rally, Kathie," Mallory began. "What did you think?"

"It was worse than I thought. You were so degrading yourself. At first, I was sure I had to break up with you. But then I liked you throwing cats at the C-Team."

"If I quit the campaign, Lou will probably fire me."

"You *will* quit the campaign. You already told me and Anne. You have to get away from those scum."

*** ***

Anne soon came back from the parking lot. She was tapping like crazy on her phone, and a little out of breath. "De Santo finally made it to the stage. They said he didn't last long. He still looked deathly pale. White as a ghost, they said." She hesitated, then gave him that confident, professional stare that always made him feel like she knew best. "And, Mr. Mallory, I took you at your word. I told his campaign manager that you quit." He could tell by the set of her eyes that she was bracing for a protest, but he said nothing. "The vice presidency is an important position. By resigning, you gave up a once-in-a-lifetime chance. But I don't honestly think you'd have been happy there."

"Neither do I," Kathie added.

"I guess that settles it," Mallory said evenly, reaching for Kathie's hand. She gripped it hard. His vice presidency, his influencer status, his hope of ever profiting from Spike's internet postings, were all gone. UniCast was going under, and Lou would probably fire him now. He had nothing left of his former life except for Kathie. But he felt he had come out ahead.

Chapter 31: We Need Somebody to Blame

Lou called and ordered him to come into the dealership at 9:00 that morning. Mallory was terrified, but he was holding out hope that he would not be fired. As soon as he arrived, he was ushered into an inner office where he was told to sit down by two men he had never seen before. They identified themselves as FBI agents. He was disappointed that their suits were in no better shape than his.

Mallory thought neither of the two men interrogating him were up to the standards he expected of FBI agents. Neither of them was especially tall, one had a receding hairline, and the other wore glasses so thick they looked almost like goggles. Furthermore, neither one seemed as smart as Officer Selby. He relaxed completely and decided to study the patterns on their ties. He did give them credit for better ties than his own clip-on.

The two G-men looked at each other and nodded almost imperceptibly, then the one with the hair went on. "We have reason to believe you were involved in the incident that sickened presidential candidate De Santo at the rally Friday night. We are investigating it as a possible terrorist attack on his limousine."

Mallory had watched enough crime shows to know the cops tried to intimidate you into confessing to crimes you didn't commit. Apparently, the FBI was no different. That tactic wouldn't work on him, he was sure.

"We found your fingerprints on the name placards in each of the limos. We know you were involved."

"The placards? Oh, yeah. I remember now. I switched them. So what? Didn't everybody get peanut M&Ms? Is that a crime?"

"We don't know anything about peanuts. We do know that dangerous biological material was planted in the cabin air filters of a presidential candidate's limousine."

"Dangerous? Biological? Oh. Do you mean Squirdunk?"

We Need Somebody to Blame

*** ***

Questioned about the sudden departure of Kevin Mallory, his erstwhile vice-presidential candidate, who was last seen fleeing a group of supporters at the Columbia, Maryland, rally, Jake De Santo read this prepared statement:

Until recently, I had not personally viewed the video of my running mate interacting with the famous entertainer, Simone de Boudoir. In the past, I have applauded his efforts to support the business of this entrepreneurial young woman. However, I was shocked upon finally seeing the full scope of this encounter with my own eyes.

I was appalled to see Mr. Mallory wearing a Covid mask during his encounter with Ms. Boudoir. My whole campaign is a crusade against this kind of government interference in our lives. Mr. Mallory has betrayed all of our American values by wearing that mask. I cannot in good conscience have anything to do with such a man.

Mr. De Santo refused to take any questions. This reporter reached out to Mr. Mallory, who stated that that he left the campaign voluntarily after De Santo supporters refused to take the free cats he was offering. He claimed De Santo then had his supporters pull him off the stage and rough him up.

"Why didn't you tell them the real reason you quit?" Kathie questioned him on the way to UniCast the next day.

"That was the real reason."

"I mean, don't you see the big picture? You promised Anne you would drop that stuff about teachers pushing kids to go gay or trans. You were ashamed of what Macho Mallory was doing to Nell. The big picture is, you quit because you didn't believe any more all that stuff you got from *God's Truth* and all that stuff Spike was posting about Nell."

"I never thought about it like that." Then he thought about it. "I took Spike's word for everything, didn't I? Even though I knew he was a liar."

Mallory Meets His Match

*** ***

Spike was furious at De Santo dropping Mallory from the ticket. But instead of going after De Santo, he doubled down on his rants against the *Nells*. On the screen, Macho Mallory drew his own crude cartoon of a *Nell* hanging three cats from ropes tied to a chandelier, then shot her down from the screen with a laser beam emanating from his goatee.

Mallory visited the Dough and Go with Kathie and threatened to serve Spike with a cease and desist order.

"You don't have the money to hire a lawyer," Spike sneered.

"I can file a lawsuit myself. I've done it before."

"Bullshit."

Spike's characterization of Mallory's threat was correct. Mallory had impersonated a lawyer more than once before, but he had been lucky to stay out of jail for it. He wasn't about to try that again.

Kathie was sitting next to Mallory in the Dough and Go booth. She had one foot planted in the aisle as if she might need to be able to get out of there quickly. They both knew the confrontation wouldn't be pretty. She relaxed a little when she saw that Spike was shorter than her and seemed to be avoiding eye contact. She looked up when an even shorter, middle-aged man with dark, curly hair, wearing a white apron, approached the table with the attitude of someone in control.

"Spiro! You take customers' order?"

Spike stopped talking immediately and looked up, responding quickly to his father's use of his legal name. He grudgingly pulled himself out of the booth and took out a pad and stood as if ready to take their order. The shorter man then made eye contact with Kathie, shrugged almost imperceptibly, and went back behind the counter. They hadn't planned to order anything, but Mallory took the opportunity to order a cinnamon bun and coffee. Kathie just asked for a decaf coffee, if only to keep up the façade that they had come there to eat. Spike disappeared back to the kitchen.

"Who is that man?" Kathie whispered.

"Spike's father, Christos. Spike makes fun of his father all the time behind his back, but I think he's terrified of him."

"Is that why he still works here, even though he claims he's making twenty thousand a month on Macho Mallory?"

"Yep, I guess. And he's still living in his father's house."

Kathie looked skeptical. "Do you really think he's making that much money?"

"I talked to Anne about it. She said Macho Mallory is definitely an influencer, and influencers can make a lot of money. Most of his money comes from Cat-A-Tonic, I think."

"You would think the non-crazy people would point out how idiotic the stuff he's posting is."

"Oh, they do. He says there are plenty of anti-Mallory blogs: *Maladjusted Mallory, Midget-Brained Mallory, Mama Munching Mallory*. Some of them are making money, too."

Spike sat down with them again when he came back with the coffee and bun. "You have to stop this!" Kathie almost shouted. "You're hurting our friend. You're turning half the cat lovers in this country into vigilantes."

Spike seemed unperturbed. "You don't understand. I'm putting out the kind of stuff people want to hear. They're frustrated with their lives. They need me me to show them someone they can blame for that. It makes them feel good."

"And teachers? You want people to be outraged against teachers, too? And what's this crap about immigrant cafeteria workers masturbating with the kale?"

"If you followed *God's Truth*, you'd find out that all of this is true." Spike spoke slowly, as if he were teaching a slow learner.

"Why do you believe this?"

"*I* am proof of it." Spike's eyes were suddenly fiery. "I was kicked out of business school to make room for the LGBTQ-plusses. *God's Truth* was a revelation for me. It helped me find my way out of the morass I was in. It made me rich! If it wasn't for *God's Truth*, I'd still be at the back of the line. Me, a native-born, red-blooded, real American, at the back of the line!"

"Hey! Red-Blooded! Table nine! Now!"

*** ***

"News!" Kathie came to his cubicle at UniCast the next morning. "Remember Sean Forester, the guy who came to tell us this whole office is being shut down? He's been fired."

"What? Why?"

"He wasn't supposed to tell us we'd all be laid off. UniCast management wanted to keep it a secret so we would all keep working hard to maintain the customer base and the revenue stream until the moment they dropped the axe on us."

*** ***

Mallory was surprised that he wasn't fired from Lou's Lexus. He had been frightened of what Lou's reaction to the limousine fiasco would be, but Lou was nowhere to be seen when he arrived, and Rick told him to just go back to his stand and bring in some business. He sold a coolant flush and two transmission flushes to the first three customers he talked to.

Rick pulled him aside later. "Victor's been fired on account of that limo that made De Santo sick. He confessed something to the FBI." Mallory held his breath, hoping his name hadn't come up as one of the guilty parties. "Victor was trying to put Squirdunk in the cabin air filter of *your* limo, but he somehow got mixed up and put it in De Santos's instead." Mallory was relieved that the FBI hadn't

189

told Rick he'd switched the placards himself. "It's probably still some kind of crime," Rick went on, "but I don't think the FBI cares much about raccoon guts. But Lou was furious when he heard about it."

Mallory's opinion of Victor went up. Putting the remains of Squirdunk in the limousine had been a good prank. And he had no sympathy for De Santo whatsoever. De Santo was saying horrible things about teachers like Anne's mother. He was saying lesbians shouldn't be allowed to be teachers, or even to be around children at all. And he had called Mallory a government "toady" on national TV. That word especially irked him.

"Victor threw Squirdunk's guts on me last week," he mumbled to Rick's back just as the manager began to walk away. Rick stopped, turned around.

"You didn't report that. You thought you could take care of that yourself, I guess." Rick tilted his head like a dog, as if to get a better look at him. "I'm surprised you were able to hold your own like that."

Mallory froze, confused. But then he realized Rick had just given him a sort of manly compliment. He didn't know how to react to such a thing. But it didn't matter, because Rick was gone by the time he figured out what was happening.

Kathie had news when she picked him up to drive him home.

"I heard from Anne," she began. "She knows an Everdine guy who's on the board of American Values. She said she was going to talk to him."

"Any guy would talk to her."

"Hm. Well. She's planning on chatting him up to find out if there are any job openings at Everdine."

"I hope they don't hire her. I hope she gets a job working for somebody decent this time."

Kathie sighed. "Can you forget about admiring her for a minute, and listen to me? So, Anne will have this chance to talk to Everdine, privately, back-channel. She asked me if there was anything she could say to discourage Everdine from taking over UniCast."

Chapter 32: Not the Man She Thought He Was

As she drove him to UniCast the next morning, Kathie said she wanted to have a heart-to-heart talk with him. "I think I'm figuring you out. You're not used to thinking about the big picture. You only think about, like, one step ahead. That works really well when you're fighting UniCast managers who are just one step away from being fired themselves. But, Kevin, it's no way to run your whole life."

"You're saying I'm not the man you thought I was."

"Maybe not." A crushing silence seemed to smother both of them. "But you keep surprising me," she added under her breath.

Mallory pondered the meaning of this conversation all morning while his customer service phone rang unanswered. Kathie had eagerly kissed him, purred at his touch. But he had often in the past overestimated a woman's devotion to him based on a brief sexual romp. He had thought Kathie was the real thing. How could she still be deciding who he was? Had she been just trying him out? The connection they had shared so far apparently wasn't enough for her. He felt like she wanted more from him, but he didn't know what.

With the news that the whole division would be shut down, and in the absence of an immediate supervisor on the premises, a few of his fellow workers took his approach of ignoring all customer calls and congregating in the break room. Someone even brought in a ping pong net and paddles and took over half the area of that room. But to Mallory's surprise, the great majority of the workers kept their noses to the grindstone and their headpieces to their ears. Mallory thought their loyalty to the company that was laying them off was worse than stupid. But he thought he'd check his opinion against Kathie's.

"No. I agree with you," she said. "I think it's dumb. People should be spending their time looking for other jobs."

"But I'm the boss now," he said. His enigmatic tone drew her attention. "Remember how I used to figure out ways to make Harrison miserable if he didn't give me what I wanted? Why can't we figure out a way to make Everdine miserable about the whole takeover?"

*** ***

Victor was never charged with any crime by the FBI. Apparently, the odor of decomposing racoon, sickening as it was, was not actually life-threatening. And when the FBI found out that Victor's motive was to get back at Mallory for dating Kathie, they decided this was not any kind of terrorist motivation. But Lou was so angry at the chaos caused at the De Santo rally that he fired Victor and banned him from the premises.

Mallory didn't hear any talk around the shop about his switching the placards – or about his quitting the presidential race, for that matter. Apparently, Rick didn't tell Lou that Mallory had made the switch that ultimately caused De Santo to get so sick. And Mallory was surprised to find out that Rick didn't even know who De Santo was. So Mallory still had hopes of keeping this part-time job long enough to be able to buy a cheap used car.

Chapter 33: Superpower

"What's going on in this place? There's no receptionist out there. I didn't see any security guard." Anne was explaining why she had just popped into his cubicle. Mallory was glad to see her. She was one of his growing list of fantastic women who, he realized, were all out of his league. But he enjoyed just talking to her. He asked what she was doing.

"Looking for a job," she explained cheerfully. "I don't know how much longer I can keep on promoting American Values. Or De Santo. Hopefully, I can find a spot in somebody's campaign, somebody who I believe in. How are you doing?"

"You're talking to the new Acting Supervisor of Customer Service." He had to laugh at this title. Ever since Harrison had departed, Mallory had left all the managerial decisions up to Ms. Marcie. She still insisted on consulting him on all the important problems such as the ping pong table and the fact that Rhys in Building Management had not hired a new security guard.

"I have to admit I'm surprised at your promotion." Anne was nothing if not candid.

"It's nothing, honestly," Mallory admitted. "UniCast let it slip that this whole regional office is going to be closed down as part of the Everdine takeover. Nobody cares who is the manager now. People here are spending most of their time looking for other jobs, or playing gin rummy in the break room."

"Actually, I know one of the principals at Everdine. He used to be on the board of American Values. I have an appointment with him in New York tomorrow." She hesitated. "I'm looking for a job with them."

"We hate Everdine! Their takeover means everybody in this building will be out of a job."

"They actually told you that?"

"Yes. Ask Kathie. That's why people here are playing ping pong and setting off the fire alarm."

Anne seemed intrigued. She asked if it were possible that she speak to Kathie about her unit's statistical projections for UniCast. Mallory was surprised at that request, but he was happy that the two women were apparently still getting along. He started to draw her a map to Kathie's cubicle, then decided it would be easier to lead her there himself. He was also hoping to be invited into the conversation, but Anne didn't seem to think he was the person she should consult about statistics and projected cash flow.

He trudged back to his cubicle. He decided to check out the various iterations of Macho Mallory to see what Spike was up to. He was surprised to see the little cartoon caricature now chasing other little cartoon characters around and ripping off their masks. The *Nell* postings were becoming even more creative. Spike was providing the C-Teams with information on how to spot cat abusers. Anyone with gay or lesbian inclinations, and all women over forty, were presumed to be in that category. These abusers were now supposedly practicing human-cat copulation. The comments after these posts showed many readers believed this was true. Mallory knew from his own direct observation that Nell loved her cats and would never do anything to harm them. He clicked off and changed to *God's Truth*. He no longer believed everything on that website either. If Anne's mother was a teacher, and if Anne said teachers were not indoctrinating kids, that was good enough for him. He appreciated for the first time how important it was to have real friends to help him figure out what was true from what was false.

He heard a quick clacking of heels in the corridor and turned to see his two friends, Anne and Kathie, standing side by side in his cubicle opening. The two women exchanged hesitant glances. Finally, Kathie stepped in, leaned close. "There's been a shooting on Nell's street."

"Oh my God!"

"Shh. We're not sure of anything yet. But we should go – don't you think?"

Mallory Meets His Match

*** **

A police car was blocking the road. They weren't the first people to pull onto the shoulder and gawk. They could see more police cars ahead on Nell's street. Because Anne had insisted on going with them, Mallory had ridden lying down in the bed of Kathie's tiny truck. Now he stood up and got a better view of the house than either of the two women.

"It's definitely Nell's house," he reported. "There's some SWAT team guys with their machine guns and all, standing on either side of her front door. There's somebody with a bullhorn, talking."

More police cars arrived, and the officers started moving people even further back from the house. "That's my friend," Mallory yelled in protest. "She's in there."

"She's in there alright," the cop shouted back even as Kathie started to turn her truck around. "She's in there with a rifle. A loaded rifle. A loaded rifle she already shot once. Just get back!"

Most of the other spectators drove away as soon as they were shooed back out of sight of the house. Kathie said they could probably see everything better on the TV news anyway, but Mallory said no. "We've got to do something now. You see, Anne, we have to. We gave her that rifle."

Anne seemed to shrink away from them at this news.

"We were trying to help her," Kathie explained quickly. "She had a sick dog with cancer. She had to put it down. The vets refused to do it. The county refused to do it. And nobody else would help her. I guess we should've gotten the rifle back."

Mallory hung his head. "The C-Team probably came after her. I just hope nobody got killed."

"... with your gun." Anne's look was accusatory as she finished his thought.

Mallory's face went slack. His friend Officer Selby had tried to teach him to think ahead about the consequences of his actions. He'd done the opposite. He'd left his gun with a woman who was already on the edge and who was being harassed daily by her neighbors. And that harassment was mostly his fault, too. It didn't seem to Mallory like he would ever measure up to Selby's standards, much less to Anne's or Kathie's. All he could do now was hope the worst hadn't already happened.

Anne interrupted his spasm of despair. "You guys know her? There must be something we can do."

But they couldn't think of anything. They were so far away they could barely see the roof of the house. Mallory stood on the truck bed again. He saw yet another police car coming their way. It stopped right next to the truck. When the officer got out, he saw it was Officer Selby himself.

"Mr. Mallory," Selby began. "Corporal Benson told me someone in your truck is a friend of Nell Pickens, the woman holed up in that house."

"She's alive?" Mallory felt a rush of relief.

"Yeah. Let me explain. We have a standoff at the house. A neighbor complained that Ms. Pickens was standing on her front porch with a rifle and shot it in the air when she came close."

"Is that a crime?" Mallory's litigious instincts instantly kicked in.

Selby ignored the question. "She won't come outside to talk to us. She's threatening to shoot herself if we enter the house. She claims the neighbors have formed a secret pact to lynch her at sundown. She's just not making any sense. If any of the three of you think you can talk to her, maybe you can calm her down. That's why I'm here."

Kathie and Mallory looked at each other. It wasn't a question of which one of them was closer to Nell. It was a question of which one she hated the least. Mallory felt that he probably held that title. "I've done awful things to Nell, but I've never broken her heart. I could never hurt her as much as you did. I'm going." Kathie opened her mouth as if to say something, but Mallory turned to go before she could find her words.

"If she comes out of that door with that rifle, she's dead." Selby was coaching Mallory on their way to the house. "We don't want that to happen. You're going to stand behind the fire truck and talk through the bullhorn first. Try to get her to put the rifle on the ground and kick it out to us."

"Can't I just say it's my rifle and I want it back?"

Shelby's look forced Mallory to think. "Sorry." Mallory picked up the bullhorn. He had trouble understanding how it worked, and the first sound that came out of it startled him so badly he dropped it. "Sorry. But why can't we just call her?"

"She's turned off her phone."

"Well, this thing isn't going to work." He shoved the bullhorn aside with his foot, walked past Selby, around the fire truck and towards the door. Selby shouted after him to stop. The two SWAT team members at the door turned their machine guns on him. He heard Selby behind him yelling for them to hold up. He walked right between the two SWAT team members and knocked on the door.

"Who is it?" Her voice sounded so surprisingly casual and musical one of the SWAT team members snorted a quiet laugh.

"Um, this is Kevin Mallory, Nell." He thought he'd get to the point. "They say you've gone off the deep end."

"They want to take away Florence and Kiki and Brute." Her voice was tiny behind the closed door.

"No they don't. They want to take *you* away."

"I'm not leaving my animals."

"You've been through a lot. They say you need treatment or counselling or something."

"The neighbors, and the C-Teams, they're coming to take my animals."

"You need to come with me. I'm afraid these assholes out here are going to shoot you."

"I'd rather die than give up Florence or Kiki or Brute."

There had never been a moment in his life when Mallory had

felt more certain that he was in the right place at the right time. "You don't have to die. You don't have to give up your animals. You know somebody who can take care of Florence and Kiki and Brute, don't you? Admit it."

Her response was muffled.

"Was that a *yes*? Knock one time if that was a *yes*."

One knock.

"Right, Nell. I can do it. I've done it before. When I had Koko, I kept him in tip-top shape."

"You did." The voice seemed to have a little more conviction behind it.

"I can take care of Florence and Kiki and Brute. These assholes at the door want to shoot you, but there's a nice cop here, Selby, and he promised me he'd get you help."

"Not the Healing Hearts."

"No. No. Someplace way better than that, I promise."

"Florence and Kiki and Brute. Will you love them, all of them?"

"I promise."

"You and nobody else?"

"Just me. I promise. Can you come out now?"

Nell's silence went on for so long Mallory began to despair. Taking care of cats was maybe the only thing in his life he was really good at. It was his only superpower. He figured he could do a dog, too, for a short time, if he had to. But his superpower would be worthless if he couldn't save Nell's life.

"Nell, can you come out now?"

The door opened slowly. She stuck her head out, looked only at him.

"Okay."

*** ***

Mallory, Kathie and Anne huddled in a corner of the UniCast break room that evening, long after quitting time. Kathie clicked off her conversation with Officer Selby.

"Nell's been committed for at least thirty days."

"This day has been the last straw," Anne sighed. "There's too much sick stuff going on, and American Values is just making things worse. I'm going to quit."

"You had nothing to do with this," Kathie insisted. "It was Mallory's friend who invented the *Nell* thing that hurt her so much. And Mallory went along with it for a while. They made money off of it."

"Oh, that's awful. The whole thing's awful," Anne sympathized. "And I'm sorry for you guys, too."

"We saw Nell a lot." Kathie admitted. "She told us what was happening to her. Now that I think back on it, we sometimes laughed at her behind her back."

"I don't think you should blame yourselves for this. You were trying to help her, mostly. People who have breakdowns usually have an underlying problem. It's never just one thing."

"Spike and I were selling outrage." Mallory was finally feeling the full weight of responsibility for what he had done. "Outrage paid good money. Like Spike, like everybody else, I pretended there was no cost to that. But there was a cost to Nell. And who knows how many other *Nells* there are out there."

Anne said she was tired and was going back to her hotel to rest. "This has been a tough day for all of us. Maybe the one bright spot for me has been getting to know you two. Even if we never meet again …."

"If it weren't for you," Kathie interrupted, "I would still believe that all people involved in politics are scum."

Anne smiled. "I wouldn't be in politics if I thought they were all scum. But I learned a lot today. From now on, I'm going to be more careful about who I hitch my wagon to." She stood up to leave, then stopped, leaned down, and gave Mallory a quick, awkward caress. "You did a brave thing today."

Mallory was in shock. "Um, okay." He started breathing again once she was no longer touching him. He hoped Kathie wouldn't be upset. He felt that Anne really was on their side, on both of their sides. He tried to think of the appropriate way to tell her, in the exact right words, right in front of Kathie, what a good person he thought she was. But that was too scary. Words failed him. He watched as Kathie stood up and they gave each other brief, girlie hugs. Anne turned to go. He had to say *something*.

"Anne, do us a favor. When you interview with that Everdine guy tomorrow, put in a bad word for us."

Chapter 34: Outrage is Our Brand

"It's his fault," Kathie said. "He's not getting away with it." They were in the Dough and Go, which now seemed like enemy territory. Spike had brushed off their pleas to lay off Nell; instead, he had doubled down.

Police cover up mass pet murder!

The original Nell, our avatar of animal animosity, yesterday butchered her own dogs and cats for resisting her perverted sexual advances. She was taken into custody by police on Thursday. The police, on orders from the government, stood by until the mass animal slaughter was complete and only approached Nell after her AR-15 was out of ammunition.

Patriotic cat lovers should remember the danger that armed Nells pose in their neighborhoods and would be well advised to pack heat wherever they go. Don't count on the police. Those pussies are not interested in enforcing any laws except for issuing speeding tickets to law abiding citizens like you.

Our thanks to the Cat-A-Tonic people for supporting these important public messages for all true cat lovers. I wouldn't let my cats go a single day without their nutritious Cat-A-Tonic supplement.

"Did you talk to Spike about that?"

"He said what he always says. 'Outrage is our brand.' Did you bring your laptop?"

Kathie brought out her laptop, where she had stored the most outrageous of Spike's posts over the last few months. She went to the counter and motioned to Spike's father, Christos. The little man rushed to the counter, his face creased with concern.

"Something wrong with the food?"

"Something's wrong, but not with the food. Come talk with me for a minute." Kathie stood up and ushered him away from the table.

Mallory was disappointed that she left him sitting in a booth near the front of the restaurant where he could not hear what they were saying. Spike did a double take when he came out of the kitchen in the back and passed the booth where Kathie was conferring with his father. Spike's long, sideways look at his father threw him almost completely off balance. He stumbled, then recovered, then managed to bring the food back to Mallory, but he didn't sit down. He opened his mouth like he was about to say something, but then froze. Mallory had to take the dinner plates out of his hands. Spike didn't say anything, just turned and went to sit by himself at the counter.

Kathie stood up from the booth at the back of the restaurant. Mallory saw Christos holding the laptop now. Mallory stretched his neck and got a glimpse of Christos still studying the screen carefully. Spike was watching his father also. Then Christos stood up, carrying the laptop. He then walked so slowly toward his son that even Mallory was frightened.

"Spiro." Father used the son's real name. "This your work? You put this on internet?"

"*Baba*, you don't understand. Things are different here than in the old country."

"Different? Fucking with cats okay now? Picking on women? A cartoon man dancing naked with a dayglo *poutsa*? Take it down. Take it all off the internet. Today."

"You still don't understand how it works, Papa."

"I understand what a real man does. Take it down." He paused, then went on in a voice like someone pronouncing a death sentence. "You don't live in my house and say this garbage."

"You still don't understand. It's not in my name. It's …."

"Take it down or you're out of my house!"

Spike came toward their table. Kathie stood up and edged toward the door. Mallory stood up to protect her, but Spike just sat down in the booth they had just vacated and put his hands to his face. Mallory turned to catch Kathie's eye, hoping they could go. The Dough and Go seemed to go quiet, but then Kathie's eyes widened. Mallory turned back to see Christos approaching Spike. He stopped, stood over his son, slapped his hand down hard on the table. "Take it down!"

Spike jumped in his seat, looked up. He had an ugly twist to his lips that Mallory had never seen before. "I don't need your money, old man. I don't need your job. I don't need your house. Soon I'll be making more in a week than you make in a year."

The older man's hands were trembling as he held the laptop. "Out, then. Out." There was a tremor in his voice as he tried not to yell. Spike started to push himself out of the booth. "Your sister, your *mama*, your *yia-yia*, they need to see what kind of man you are. I show this to them."

"No!" Spike grabbed for the laptop, but his father stepped back, gripping it more tightly. Spike stopped, stood stock-still. His face had become pale and drawn. He seemed to shrink before their eyes. That demonic glow that had powered his internet fantasies seemed to have faded. "No. Don't tell Mom," he pleaded now. "Don't show her anything. Please. Please."

His father folded his arms around the laptop as if to contain the shame that was threatening to contaminate his whole family. Spike reached out for it with a tremulous hand. "Please. Please. That's not really the kind of man I am. I'll do what you say. I promise."

His father's eyes softened a bit. He reached around Spike and handed the laptop back to Kathie. "Take it out of my restaurant, please, ma'am." His voice went soft. "My son is finished with this *skata*." Father and son stared at each other in silence. There seemed to be one more thing to settle.

"*Mom*?" Spike's eyes were pleading.

As Christos stared at his son, his own eyes gradually softened. "Your mother," he softly growled. "She don't need to know."

Mallory and Kathie were halfway across the tiny parking lot when the Dough and Go door squished open and Spike stepped out behind them. By the time he reached them, his complexion had completely changed. All the blood that had drained out of his face before had roared back. His features were now tinged with a hellish glow. He threw himself into Mallory and knocked him into the tiny garden of the pizza parlor just across from the Dough and Go. Mallory's shins cracked hard on the rocks on the edge as he fell flat into the rosebushes. He landed with a thud, grinding himself into the stickers. But he rolled over and got up quickly rather than wallow in the pain. He was afraid for Kathie.

Spike was screaming in Kathie's face that she'd regret what she did, that he would brand her as a whore and a *Nell* all over the internet. Mallory approached him fast, the adrenaline pumping and eclipsing the pain.

"Don't worry, Kathie," he interrupted Spike's rant. "If he does that, his Daddy's gonna tell his Mommy, and he's scared of his Mommy."

Spike turned and took a wild swing at him, but Mallory ducked. Spike had to take a few steps to the side to regain his balance. Mallory moved one step toward him, and he backed up. Mallory tried another step, and Spike turned and walked away, looking back just once over his shoulder.

Mallory collapsed onto the asphalt, cradling his shins. He couldn't get any words out to tell Kathie what was wrong. She seemed mostly worried about the scratches on his face, which were starting to hurt, too. He liked her gentle touch there. He knew he had to stand up eventually. He knew she would help him.

Epilogue

Spike managed to keep the Cat-A-Tonic account by finding a new source of outrage for Macho Mallory. The new target was De Santo, who had supposedly ordered his bodyguards to beat up the real Mallory. When the flash of interest in that issue quickly faded, he provided an actual video of De Santo vomiting onto a cat cage at the recent rally. Anyone who saw that video could easily believe that De Santo then ordered all the cats to be thrown into the lake in their cages, as Spike now claimed.

De Santo's approval ratings in the polls trended slowly but inexorably downward. Spike didn't let up, and the Cat-A-Tonic money came in so fast that he could afford to fix up his father's garage into an apartment of sorts and move into it. But he had promised his father that he would lay off the more deviant allegations, and so his posts now only hinted at, and only very delicately, the various ways De Santo satisfied his fixations with animals.

The ping pong games in the UniCast break room grew more serious after betting was allowed. Mallory was distressed when Rhys, who hadn't yet gotten around to hiring a replacement security guard for the building, signed up to play and was put in one of the brackets. Mallory thought about stopping the whole thing until Kathie told him to go ahead and put his money on her ex-boyfriend. Mallory watched his first few matches and was pleased he had picked such a winner. He had previously turned over all his real supervisory duties to Ms. Marcie. In her own quiet way, she began to lecture him, saying that the ping pong tournament was unprofessional. But he couldn't see any reason to put a stop to his new, fun hobby.

He didn't know how many animals he was allowed to have in his apartment, but he decided on his own that three were probably too many. Kathie volunteered to take Brute for a few days, but he remembered he had promised Nell that he would personally take

Epilogue

care of all three animals. He had also promised he would love them, but he later decided that was a bridge too far. The cats seemed to be getting used to their new home, but that squat little Brute barked and howled at every single bird that flew by, every single car that started up, every single noise in the apartment complex parking lot. Mallory bought a wall calendar and, like a prisoner, marked off the days until Nell would be released.

Kathie was looking for a job. She told him that most of her prospects were out of state. He knew he couldn't really follow her because of his horrible employment record. He resolved to savor every minute he had left with her. He asked her over almost every night. She almost always said yes.

Everything changed when the Everdine hedge fund decided not to take over UniCast after all. The projected earnings from their regional office were so low that a takeover seemed to be a money-losing proposition. Kathie was the author of those projections, but she said they were accurate "taking into consideration the ping pong tournament, and the fact that we don't have any security, and that half the people in the Customer Assistance unit and Sales are playing video games on their computers all day." She insisted she did nothing improper, except possibly leaking the projections to Anne, who leaked them to her Everdine contact. The bottom line was that their jobs were no longer going to be eliminated.

Mallory was shocked when the Howard County Hospital called and told him that he had been listed as the emergency contact for Nell. He was even more shocked when she called. "Don't you have anybody better to be your emergency contact?" he asked right away.

"You're the one who knows how Brute and Florence and Kiki are doing. Are they okay?"

Mallory had cheated a little on his promises to Nell. He had let Kathie take Brute for a few days. He didn't see any harm in it, and he had always kept Florence and Kiki himself. Although neither of those cats had quite the charisma that Koko had once charmed him with, he grew fond of both of them. "All the animals are doing fine." He told her truthfully. "How are *you* doing, Nell?"

"I don't think I can go back to that neighborhood."

"Yes, you can, Nell. Kathie and I forced Spike to drop the *Nell* business entirely. You're not in any danger anymore."

"How *is* Kathie?"

"She's fine." He paused. "You know, she loves you. Not in *that* way, but … you know …. You should have seen how worried she was about you that day."

"Both of you guys cared. I saw that. You were the only ones. That keeps me going. Listen, I'm not telling this to anybody here. You know I wouldn't ever shoot anybody. But I thought about … when the SWAT team was there … I thought about using that gun on myself." She paused as if waiting for Mallory to respond, but he was too shocked to say anything, so she went on. "But I couldn't figure out how to do it. That rifle is so damn *long*." Mallory wasn't sure. He might have imagined it. But he thought he heard her suppress a tiny laugh.

Mallory promoted Ms. Marcie to the position of Acting Assistant Supervisor of Customer Assistance, a position he created that existed in name only. He knew that would give her a leg up on becoming the real supervisor when he resigned from that position, which he planned to do as soon as everyone realized that Everdine wasn't taking over UniCast, that the office wasn't being disbanded, and that it might be in everyone's interest to have a working Customer Assistance unit.

He confessed to Kathie that he still didn't like his job. He didn't like his job at Lou's either, and he was beginning to think there was something fishy about the way Rick was running the service department there. He told Kathie she was the only part of his life that wasn't dull, boring, aggravating or sketchy. But there actually was one exception. He enjoyed taking care of Florence and Kiki, just as he had loved taking care of Koko previously. He asked Kathie if there was any kind of job he could get taking care of cats. She responded only that there was no end to the ways he had of surprising her. He figured he'd have to find out that answer for himself.

He was excited to hear from Anne. "She didn't take the job at Everdine!" he announced one morning to Kathie. "She signed on instead as a political aide to a candidate for governor of Illinois. And she's going to stop by and see us."

"You hate politics, and you're out of it now," Kathie responded. "Why are you so thrilled about seeing her come here?"

"I don't know. I like her. She was the only real person I met in that … life."

"But you're not going to be in that life anymore, right?"

"Right." He studied her face. "Wait a minute. Are you jealous?" If she was, having a woman jealous of him would be yet another new experience for him. Kathie seemed to be providing new experiences for him all the time.

"Okay, maybe I'm a little jealous. I don't like it when your head is turned by other women." Her tone was definite, but her look was sheepish at first. Then she seemed to get herself together and revert to her usual, confident mode. "I want you all for myself," she declared flatly. "I don't want to share you." She stared at him. "So, sue me."

Printed in the USA
CPSIA information can be obtained
at www.ICGtesting.com
JSHW021149250724
66931JS00006B/81/J